satisFRY

The **Air Fryer** Cookbook

Mona Dolgov

award-winning author of *satisfy*

YOU
LIVE
RIGHT
PUBLISHERS

The information in this book is based on facts, credible
resources, and personal experiences.

Nutritional information is given as a reference and may vary due to differences
in sizes, brands and types of ingredients. Nutritional calculations were done
using multiple resources, including the USDA database, and nutritional
information provided by the most popular manufacturers of a given
food. Calories were rounded to the nearest 5 and all other amounts were
rounded to the nearest 0.5 of a gram. Net carbohydrates were calculated
by subtracting fiber grams from the grams of total carbohydrates.

This information is not intended to diagnose, prevent, treat, or cure any disease.
The author and publisher will in no event be held liable for any loss or other
damages, including but not limited to special, incidental, consequential, or
any other damages. The advice in this book is intended for otherwise healthy
individuals and should not take priority over advice from a doctor. Please
consult your doctor before making any changes to the way you eat.

The author's reference to various brands does not imply endorsement or
sponsorship. Product names are the trademarks of their respected owners.

Published by You Live Right, LLC, Boston, MA 02210
www.youliveright.com

Editorial Director: Mona Dolgov
Editors: Christian Stella, Wendy Martin-Shuma,
Abe Ogden, Scott Dolgov, Mona Dolgov
Food Photography: Christian and Elise Stella
Lifestyle Photography: Allan Dines
Book Design: Christian Stella
Recipe Development and Testing: Mona Dolgov, Christian Stella
Nutritional Advisor: Mona Dolgov

Library of Congress Control Number: 2022905907
ISBN: 978-1-7366756-1-8

First Edition
10 9 8 7 6 5 4 3 2 1

Printed in Canada

table of contents

Introduction

The Air Fryer, My New "Mona-vation"

My "Monavation" is to make healthier, nutritious meals that nourish, satisfy, and make life easier. I believe the air fryer can help achieve these goals and it has truly changed the way I cook! If you have my last book, *satisfy*, you know that all of my recipes are gluten-free, nutritious, packed with vegetables, and made in "full-filling" portions to get you through your day. Those things haven't changed in this book; the air fryer has simply allowed me to prepare recipes FASTER, and with even tastier results!

I've spent the last two years finding new and exciting ways to use my air fryers (I have a few different air fryers now to make sure my recipes work for everyone) and have consulted with my wonderful community for new ideas that can make air frying a cornerstone of how you cook.

I've created this cookbook to give you all the confidence you need to air fry healthier meals in minutes! I've developed and tested recipes for every occasion, with a wide range of proteins, vegetables, and cuisines to suit every taste. I've even included extra tips throughout to make your life a little easier and ensure consistent results. Whether it's a satisfying snack, a complete meal for two, or a healthy-delicious and perfectly-portioned dessert, I hope this book will make the air fryer your new kitchen obsession as well!

This book can show you that the air fryer isn't just about making French fries (although it can make some good fries). I'm hoping I can motivate you to eat more veggies and lean proteins to create complete and balanced meals. With the right recipes, we can all live a healthier lifestyle. Even more important, we can maintain and enjoy that lifestyle for a lifetime!

As a nutritionist, I use nutrient-dense ingredients and simple food swaps to create heart-healthy recipes that follow Mediterranean diet principles. All of the recipes are gluten-free and plant-forward, using real ingredients. You will still find lean meats and even sweet desserts, but it's all about balance. It's about eating more of the healthier foods that make us feel great!

Creating simple, satisfying, and nutritious meals to transform lives is my passion. The air fryer is just the tool to help make this a reality. You will be amazed at the simplicity and the cooking results. I'm so excited to share all of it with you in *satisfry*.

Hugs, Mona

SPECIAL THANKS

This book wouldn't be named **satisfry** without the suggestion of one of my air fryer cooking students, and friend, Phil Adler. He suggested it in one of my classes and it stuck!

Many thanks to my whole team, friends, and **satisfy** community, who embraced my cooking principles and helped make this book happen, while providing great inspiration, motivation, and ideas every step of the way.

I especially want to thank Christian Stella and his wife Elise, who worked with me to create amazing recipes and then made them come to life with beautiful food photography.

Thanks to Lane Wilson, for her creative marketing designs and Allan Dines for fun lifestyle photography.

I want to thank my loving family for all of your support and patience. Rachel and Scotty, I LOVE cooking with you. Whether it is a holiday meal, or a summer cook-a-long in Martha's Vineyard, we always have smiles, laughter, fun, and comfort in the kitchen. Rachel, you are a pro at those Eggplant Stackers, chicken burgers, and tacos (and Adam is a lucky guy to have you as his soon-to-be wife)! Scotty, you always inspire me with all of your Middle Eastern and Mediterranean dishes. I love the way you discover new flavors and spices and are unafraid to give them a try. The two of you really get the love of cooking and that makes me so happy!

Doug, you are always there for me—listening, tasting, testing, chopping, and cooking alongside me. You are the best and you've become an air fryer maven as well! You are my rock and my support. Thank you for your love and believing in me, and for reminding me that what I do everyday truly makes a difference.

And Mom and Dad, your spirits are always with me, telling me to keep following my dreams. I see you smiling with your knowing grins.

TEN REASONS TO LOVE YOUR AIR FRYER!

♥ **Faster cooking!** No need to preheat the oven, saving you 15 minutes every time you cook! Plus, the actual cooking time in the air fryer is around 20% faster than a conventional oven.

♥ **Less fat!** I love the fact that you get crispy results using minimal oil! A simple spritz, or a tablespoon of olive or avocado oil, at most, is all you need. In fact, air fryers work best with less oil—the fan will simply push off excess oil if added.

♥ **Less mess!** I love to prepare full meals in my air fryer, which is why I have a full chapter on them in this book! There's fewer dishes getting dirty and I can simply give my air fryer basket a quick rinse and run the air fryer for 1 minute to dry.

♥ **Even heating!** Thanks to the air circulation inside the air fryer I no longer have to worry about unevenly browned foods. Many of the recipes in this book don't even require flipping!

♥ **Set and forget!** It's so great to place dinner in the air fryer, set the timer, and simply walk away!

♥ **Your second oven!** When preparing foods on the stovetop or in a conventional oven, the air fryer makes a great second oven for an extra side dish. It's especially useful on holidays or when entertaining!

♥ **A healthy snack machine!** The air fryer is perfect for making after-work or after-school snacks! It's especially great for making small batches of snacks whenever you want them.

♥ **The best way to reheat!** Move over microwave, the air fryer has quickly become my go-to machine for reheating leftovers. It is also great for breathing new life into (healthy!) takeout food that's cooled on the way home.

♥ **Cook from frozen!** The air fryer is great for cooking frozen ingredients, as the fan quickly pushes off any extra moisture to defrost and cook at the same time!

♥ **Endless variety!** Whether it's a shakshuka breakfast or a perfectly-portioned dessert, the recipes in this cookbook can show you that the air fryer is far more versatile than just traditional "fried" foods. It is capable of making just about any nutritious and satisfying dish you can imagine.

TYPES OF AIR FRYERS

There are dozens of air fryer models available on the market. This is why I've included a range of cook times for my recipes. Due to different sizes, functions, wattages, and designs, no two air fryer models are exactly alike. I've done my best to ensure that the recipes in this book will work with any air fryer; however, you may want to take note of your cook times as you prepare the first few recipes. If your dishes are consistently cooking on the lower or higher end of my cook time range, that will likely be the case for all of the recipes in the book.

Bucket-Style

The original air fryer models were all bucket-style, with an oval shape on the outside and a deep frying basket. It's a great shape for maximum air flow around the food and, depending on the wattage, will typically cook food the fastest. I highly recommend a larger model, sometimes called "XL" or "Family-Size." Otherwise, you may need to cook many recipes in multiple batches.

Sheet Pan–Style

Sheet pan–style air fryers can be very convenient, also acting as both a toaster oven and a broiler. They are often wide enough to fit a large quantity of food in a single layer, but may not be tall enough to cook larger foods like a whole chicken. If your sheet pan air fryer came included both a basket with holes and a solid sheet pan, I recommend cooking the recipes in this book using the basket. The sheet pan can be convenient to clean, but does not allow air flow to cook the food from the bottom, which may lead to longer cook times.

Other Air Fryers

Air fryers with multiple baskets side by side or multiple sheet pans stacked are also available. If your machine has extra room, the best rule of thumb is to disperse the food evenly across the most surface area. There are also combination pressure cooker/air fryers and air fryers built into full-size ovens. All of the recipes in **satisfry** can be used for all of these appliances. Simply work with the time ranges provided.

Should You Preheat an Air Fryer?

For countertop air fryers, the recipes in this book do NOT require preheating beforehand. I have found that preheating makes little, if any, difference to the final dish, as most air fryers come up to full temperature within 1 minute of starting. The only time I would recommend preheating is for foods that cook in 5 minutes or less. If you have a full-size oven with an air fryer function, consult your manual about preheating.

AIR FRYER ACCESSORIES

To get the most out of your air fryer, and the recipes in this book, I recommend a few inexpensive accessories. All of these accessories are readily available online, but many of them can also be found in large stores, in the air fryer/kitchen appliance section.

7-Inch Baking Dish

A baking dish that fits in your air fryer basket is an absolute must-have! There are many sold specifically for air fryers that range from 6.5 to 8.5 inches wide. Anything within this range will work with my recipes. Just be sure to measure the width of your inner air fryer basket before purchasing. I recommend a nonstick baking dish with a metal handle, as these are easiest to get in and out of the air fryer and easiest to clean. That said, any metal, oven-safe ceramic, or heat-treated glass (Pyrex) dish will work, as long as it is rated for over 400°F.

Metal Rack

If you have a bucket-style air fryer, I recommend buying a metal rack that you can place over food in the basket to cook in a second layer. Bucket-style air fryers are deep, but can have limited surface area at the bottom of the basket, so a metal rack can be especially helpful for cooking proteins above the vegetables. This is generally not needed if you have a wider, sheet pan–style air fryer or air fryer with multiple baskets.

6-Ounce Ramekins

Ramekins are a great way to make portion-perfect baked goods in the air fryer. The recipes in this book were tested using 6-ounce ramekins. Ceramic is classic, and my choice, but heat-treated glass (Pyrex) ramekins or jars are also available, as long as they are rated for over 400°F.

Silicone Baking Cups

Silicone baking cups are another great way to make baked goods in your air fryer and I just love their reusability! Foil or foil-lined disposable baking cups can also be used.

Silicone Egg Bite Mold

This thing is great! It allows you to make mini egg bite omelets but can also be used to make mini cheesecakes and other baked goods!

Spice Things Up with My Custom Spice Blends

Spice blends are a great way to add flavor without extra calories. Simply add a dash to your favorite lean proteins or vegetables to transform your meal. A dash of a different blend can change an entire recipe, creating an entirely new flavor profile!

Roasting Spice Blend

Great for poultry, pork, eggs, and root vegetables, such as carrots and potatoes!

INGREDIENTS

1 $^1/_2$ tablespoons paprika

1 tablespoon turmeric

1 tablespoon crushed rosemary

$^1/_2$ tablespoon dried thyme

$^1/_2$ tablespoon garlic powder

$^1/_2$ tablespoon black pepper

Chili Spice Blend

Great for chilis (of course), Southwestern dishes, sweet potatoes, and popcorn!

INGREDIENTS

3 tablespoons chili powder

2 tablespoons cumin

1 $^1/_2$ tablespoons dried oregano

1 tablespoon onion powder

$^1/_2$ teaspoon ground cayenne pepper

Barbecue Spice Blend

Great for poultry, beef, potatoes, onions, and popcorn!

INGREDIENTS

3 tablespoons smoked paprika

1 1/2 tablespoons onion powder

1/2 tablespoon garlic powder

1/2 teaspoon ground cayenne pepper

Mediterranean Spice Blend

Great for seafood, poultry, eggs, tomatoes, and vegetables (especially green veggies)!

INGREDIENTS

2 tablespoons dried oregano

2 tablespoons dried basil

1 tablespoon dried marjoram

1/2 tablespoon garlic powder

1 teaspoon crushed red pepper flakes

Anytime Breakfast

Italian Shakshuka

Accessory: 7-inch baking dish · Active Prep Time: 10 mins · Cook Time: 24 mins · Serves: 2

My son Scott introduced me to Shakshuka, an amazing Israeli breakfast of eggs poached in a tomato-based sauce filled with veggies. With a simple change in spice blends, you can create an Italian version! This meal packs a ton of nutrient-dense ingredients, and I love eating it any time of day!

INGREDIENTS

1 medium zucchini, chopped

$1/2$ bell pepper, chopped

$1/4$ red onion, chopped

1 teaspoon olive oil

1 teaspoon Mediterranean Spice Blend (see page 11)

$1/4$ teaspoon salt

$1/4$ teaspoon pepper

1 cup prepared marinara sauce

2 tablespoons chopped fresh basil

2 large eggs

3 tablespoons shredded Parmesan cheese

Mona's Tips

Heating the marinara sauce for 2 minutes before adding the eggs helps cook the bottom of the egg, similar to preheating a pan.

DIRECTIONS

1 Place zucchini, bell pepper, and onion in a 7-inch baking dish. Add olive oil, spice blend, salt, and pepper and toss to evenly coat the vegetables.

2 Place baking dish in the air fryer basket. Toss vegetables halfway through cook time.

400°F air fry 12 mins

3 Stir in marinara sauce and basil, return dish to the air fryer basket, and reduce temperature.

325°F air fry 3 mins

4 Use a spoon to make 2 divots in the vegetables and sauce before cracking an egg into each. Top all with shredded Parmesan cheese and return dish to the air fryer basket.

325°F air fry 7–9 mins

5 Remove from air fryer once the whites of the eggs have set. Serve immediately.

Calories per serving: 220 · Fat: 12.5g · Net Carbs: 12g · Fiber: 4g · Sugars: 8.5g · Protein: 13g

Hard-Boiled Eggs

Active Prep Time: 1 min · Cook Time: 16 mins · Serves: 4–8

Hard-boiled eggs in an air fryer?! You bet! The vortex of hot air inside an air fryer surrounds eggs to cook them evenly, just as they would in boiling water. Not only is it faster than boiling in water (as you don't have to wait for the water to come to a boil), I also find that the dry heat makes the shells easier to peel.

INGREDIENTS

4–8 large eggs, cold

Mona's Tips

As air fryer models do vary, I recommend that the first time you air fry hard-boiled eggs you start by only transferring 1 egg to the ice water to then peel and check for doneness. This way you can continue cooking the remaining eggs an additional minute or two, if needed. Make a note of the time that worked for your air fryer and you'll get perfect results in the future!

DIRECTIONS

1 Carefully place eggs in the air fryer basket.

2 For creamier yolks, cook 15 minutes. For firmer yolks, cook 16 minutes.

275°F   air fry   15–16 mins

3 Using tongs or an oven glove, transfer eggs to a bowl of ice water and let rest at least 1 minute.

4 Peel and serve as is, or use in your favorite recipes. Store refrigerated.

Calories per serving: 70 · Fat: 5g · Net Carbs: 0g · Fiber: 0g · Sugars: 0g · Protein: 6g

Banana Blueberry Baked Oatmeal Muffins

Accessory: 6 silicone baking cups · Active Prep Time: 10 mins · Cook Time: 12 mins · Serves: 6

Portable oatmeal, for real! These fruit- and walnut-filled muffins are exactly like having a hearty bowl of oatmeal! I love the natural sweetness of the banana and blueberries, but if you want, you can give them a small drizzle of maple syrup! Two muffins make a great meal.

INGREDIENTS

Avocado oil spray

1 cup rolled oats

1 teaspoon baking powder

$1/2$ teaspoon ground cinnamon

Pinch salt

1 medium banana, peeled

$1/4$ cup unsweetened applesauce

1 large egg

1 tablespoon nut butter, any type

$1/2$ cup blueberries

$1/4$ cup chopped walnuts

Mona's Tips

I love these muffins when warmed. To reheat, simply remove from the refrigerator and place in the air fryer at 300°F for 3–4 minutes.

DIRECTIONS

1 Lightly spray 6 silicone baking cups with avocado oil spray.

2 In a food processor, process oats until fully ground into an oat flour around the consistency of whole-wheat flour. Transfer to a mixing bowl and fold in baking powder, cinnamon, and salt.

3 In the empty food processor, process banana, applesauce, egg, and nut butter until smooth.

4 Fold the banana mixture into the oats until a thick batter has formed. Fold in blueberries and walnuts.

5 Evenly fill the 6 baking cups with the batter. For the nicest presentation, top each with a few extra blueberries and a sprinkling of whole rolled oats. Place baking cups in the air fryer basket.

325°F air fry 10–12 mins

6 Muffins are done when they have puffed up in the center and are springy to the touch. Serve warm, drizzled with pure maple syrup if you prefer added sweetness. Store refrigerated.

Calories per serving: 140 · Fat: 6.5g · Net Carbs: 15g · Fiber: 3g · Sugars: 4.5g · Protein: 4.5g

Smoked Salmon Egg Cups

Accessory: 2 ramekins · Active Prep Time: 5 mins · Cook Time: 12 mins · Serves: 2

Far easier than a poached egg, I love to air fry whole eggs in ceramic ramekins in flavorful and fun ways! This particular recipe has smoked salmon on the bottom and crumbled goat cheese, capers, and dill on top. The best part is that the edges of the salmon crisp up like bacon after air frying.

INGREDIENTS

Avocado oil spray

2 thin slices smoked salmon or lox

2 large eggs

1 rounded tablespoon crumbled goat cheese

2 teaspoons capers, drained and rinsed

2 teaspoons chopped fresh dill

Mona's Tips

There should be enough room in most air fryers to fit 4 ramekins and double this recipe. Simply add 2 minutes to the cook time.

DIRECTIONS

1 Lightly spray 2 ramekins with avocado oil spray.

2 Line the bottom and sides of the ramekins with a slice of smoked salmon. You may need to trim or fold the slices to fit depending on their size.

3 Crack an egg over the salmon in each ramekin and sprinkle with an equal amount of the crumbled goat cheese. Place ramekins in the air fryer basket.

300°F   air fry   10–12 mins

4 Cook just until whites have set.

5 Serve topped with capers and chopped fresh dill.

Calories per serving: 110 · Fat: 8g · Net Carbs: 0.5g · Fiber: 0g · Sugars: 0g · Protein: 9.5g

"Grilled" Almond Butter Sandwich

Active Prep Time: 5 mins · Cook Time: 10 mins · Serves: 1

Air fryers make a great "grilled" sandwich that is crispy and perfectly toasted without the bread flattening out as it often does in a skillet. This recipe stuffs the sandwich with almond butter, bananas, and strawberries, but you can use the same method and cook time with any nut butter and your choice of fresh fruit.

INGREDIENTS

2 tablespoons almond butter

2 slices gluten-free bread

$^1/_2$ small banana, sliced

2 strawberries, sliced

Avocado oil spray

Mona's Tips

I find that there's no need to flip the sandwich as it cooks. It does get slightly more golden brown on the top than the bottom, but it's plenty crispy and tastes great.

DIRECTIONS

1 Spread almond butter on both slices of bread.

2 Arrange the sliced banana and strawberries over the almond butter on one slice of bread. Top with the remaining slice of bread to create a sandwich.

3 Lightly spray both sides of the sandwich with avocado oil spray and place in the air fryer basket.

350°F   air fry   8–10 mins

4 Cook just until golden brown.

Calories per serving: 340 · Fat: 18g · Net Carbs: 31g · Fiber: 8g · Sugars: 11g · Protein: 12g

Spinach and Artichoke Frittata

Accessory: 7-inch baking dish · Active Prep Time: 20 mins · Cook Time: 16 mins · Serves: 2

Like an open-faced omelet, frittatas get a beautiful and golden-brown top in the air fryer. Spinach, artichokes, and mushrooms are a favorite for frittata fillings, especially when topped with shredded Parmesan cheese!

INGREDIENTS

Olive oil spray

$^3/_4$ cup sliced baby
  bella mushrooms

3 cups fresh spinach

1 teaspoon Mediterranean
  Spice Blend (see page 11)

2 large eggs

4 large egg whites

$^1/_4$ teaspoon salt

$^1/_8$ teaspoon baking powder

$^1/_8$ teaspoon garlic powder

$^1/_8$ teaspoon pepper

4 ounces quartered marinated
  artichoke hearts, drained

3 tablespoons shredded
  Parmesan cheese

1 Roma tomato, diced

Mona's Tips

This same method can be used to make any type of frittata with your favorite fillings!

DIRECTIONS

1 Spray a skillet with olive oil spray and place on the stove over medium-high heat. Add mushrooms and sauté 7 minutes, until they begin to cook down.

2 Add spinach and spice blend and sauté 3 additional minutes, just until spinach has wilted. Drain well of any excess liquid and let cool at least 5 minutes.

3 In a mixing bowl, whisk together eggs, egg whites, salt, baking powder, garlic powder, and pepper.

4 Spray a 7-inch baking dish with olive oil spray. Add the cooked mushrooms and spinach, as well as the artichoke hearts. Stir in whisked egg mixture and ensure the vegetables are evenly dispersed.

5 Top with the shredded Parmesan cheese and transfer baking dish to the air fryer basket.

325°F   air fry   14–16 mins

6 Frittata is done when golden brown and springy to the touch. Serve sliced and topped with chopped Roma tomato.

Calories per serving: 245 · Fat: 14.5g · Net Carbs: 4g · Fiber: 3g · Sugars: 2g · Protein: 19.5g

French Toast Sticks

Active Prep Time: 10 mins · Cook Time: 12 mins · Serves: 2

These dippable sticks can be made with your choice of healthful and gluten-free bread, whether it is whole-grain or gluten-free. There's enough flavor and sweetness in the batter (thanks to pure maple syrup, cinnamon, and vanilla) to eat them all on their own, but they're even better when served with my 2-ingredient maple yogurt dipping sauce!

INGREDIENTS

Avocado oil spray

1 large egg

1 large egg white

1 tablespoon plain nonfat Greek yogurt

$1/2$ tablespoon pure maple syrup

$1/4$ teaspoon vanilla extract

$1/4$ teaspoon ground cinnamon

Pinch salt

2 slices gluten-free bread

Maple Yogurt Dipping Sauce

$1/4$ cup plain nonfat Greek yogurt

1 tablespoon pure maple syrup

Mona's Tips

Depending on the size of your bread (many gluten-free brands are quite small), you may be able to fit sticks from 3 slices in your air fryer basket.

DIRECTIONS

1 Spray the air fryer basket with avocado oil spray.

2 In a shallow bowl, whisk together egg, egg white, Greek yogurt, maple syrup, vanilla extract, cinnamon, and salt.

3 Slice bread into $3/4$-inch-wide sticks and dip into the egg mixture, flipping to coat well. Transfer to the air fryer basket in a single layer. Lightly spray the tops of the French toast sticks with avocado oil spray.

4 Flip French toast sticks 6 minutes into the cook time.

375°F   air fry   10–12 mins

5 Cook just until lightly browned.

6 Meanwhile, prepare the maple yogurt dipping sauce by combining Greek yogurt and maple syrup. Serve alongside the French toast sticks.

Calories per serving: 170 · Fat: 3.5g · Net Carbs: 23.5g · Fiber: 2.5g · Sugars: 11g · Protein: 9g

Sweet Potato and Sausage Hash

Accessory: metal rack · Active Prep Time: 15 mins · Cook Time: 22 mins · Serves: 4

This hearty breakfast hash starts with crispy air fried sweet potatoes as a base and adds kale, bell pepper, and onion for more flavor, color, and nutrition. For protein, you can add your choice of turkey, chicken, or plant-based breakfast sausage. For even more protein, top with a poached or over-easy egg.

INGREDIENTS

1 large sweet potato

2 teaspoons olive oil

1 bell pepper, chopped

$1/2$ red onion, chopped

Olive oil spray

1 teaspoon paprika

$1/4$ teaspoon onion powder

$1/4$ teaspoon salt

$1/4$ teaspoon pepper

3 cups chopped fresh kale

1 tablespoon chopped fresh sage

8 links fully cooked turkey, chicken, or plant-based breakfast sausage, thawed if frozen

Mona's Tips

This can be simplified to a side dish of home fries by tossing only the chopped sweet potato in the olive oil and spices. Air fry at 400°F for 16–18 minutes.

DIRECTIONS

1   Chop sweet potato into $3/4$-inch pieces. Toss in the olive oil and transfer to the air fryer basket.

400°F   air fry   8 mins

2   Add the chopped bell pepper and onion and lightly spray with olive oil spray. Season all with paprika, onion powder, salt, and pepper, and toss to coat.

400°F   air fry   8 mins

3   Add the chopped kale and sage and lightly spray with olive oil spray. Toss to evenly distribute. Chop the breakfast sausage and place over top. Place a metal rack over the food in the basket to keep the kale from blowing around.

400°F   air fry   4–6 mins

4   Hash is done when sweet potatoes are tender and sausage is beginning to brown. Toss all to evenly distribute the sausage before serving. Serve topped with a fried egg, if desired.

Calories per serving: 185 · Fat: 5g · Net Carbs: 18.5g · Fiber: 4g · Sugars: 5.5g · Protein: 14g

Mediterranean Egg Bites

Accessory: 7-cup silicone egg bite mold · Active Prep Time: 10 mins · Cook Time: 15 mins · Serves: 7

Now you can make your own version of famous coffeehouse egg bites at home! All you need is a silicone egg bite mold that fits perfectly in an air fryer. My Mediterranean version has my favorite combo of spinach, sun-dried tomatoes, and feta cheese. You are going to LOVE making these!

INGREDIENTS

Olive oil spray

$1/3$ cup frozen chopped spinach, thawed

2 tablespoons chopped sun-dried tomatoes

2 teaspoons chopped fresh oregano

5 large eggs

$1/4$ cup crumbled feta cheese

$1/4$ teaspoon garlic powder

$1/8$ teaspoon salt

Mona's Tips

Your favorite vegetables, proteins, and/or cheese can be substituted in place of the spinach, sun-dried tomatoes, oregano, and feta cheese to make your own egg bites. Crunchy vegetables should be sautéed until tender and then cooled before adding.

DIRECTIONS

1   Lightly spray a 7-cup silicone egg bite mold with olive oil spray. Press the spinach between paper towels to remove any excess water.

2   Evenly distribute the spinach, sun-dried tomatoes, and oregano between the 7 egg bite cups.

3   Crack 1 large egg in a food processor or blender. Add the feta cheese and pulse until entirely smooth. Add the remaining 4 eggs, garlic powder, and salt and pulse just until all is scrambled and combined.

4   Pour the egg mixture evenly over the spinach and tomatoes in the 7 egg bite cups. Gently stir each bite to disperse the spinach. Place egg bites mold in the air fryer basket.

275°F   air fry   13–15 mins

5   Egg bites are done when the centers begin to puff up and are springy to the touch. Serve warm.

Calories per serving: 70 · Fat: 4.5g · Net Carbs: 1.5g · Fiber: 0.5g · Sugars: 0.5g · Protein: 5.5g

Granola, Fruit, and Yogurt Bowls

Active Prep Time: 15 mins · Cook Time: 8 mins · Serves: 4

The air fryer can make wonderfully crisp homemade granola from only a handful of all-natural ingredients. It's so good that you can simply eat the granola as is as a grab-and-go snack or you can make it the star of a Granola, Fruit, and Yogurt Bowl.

INGREDIENTS

Granola

1 tablespoon coconut oil, melted

1 tablespoon honey

$1/2$ teaspoon ground cinnamon

$1/4$ teaspoon vanilla extract

Pinch salt

$3/4$ cup rolled oats

$1/4$ cup chopped raw almonds

2 teaspoons ground flaxseed

Each Granola and Fruit Bowl

$3/4$ cup nonfat plain Greek yogurt

$1/4$ cup mashed berries or
   frozen acai purée, thawed

Honey, to taste

$1/4$ cup prepared granola

$1/3$ cup fresh sliced fruit

DIRECTIONS

1 Line the air fryer basket with parchment paper.

2 In a mixing bowl, whisk together melted coconut oil, honey, cinnamon, vanilla extract, and salt.

3 Fold in rolled oats, almonds, and flaxseed. Press onto the parchment paper in the air fryer basket in a thick layer. Toss granola halfway through cooking.

325°F   air fry   8 mins

4 Once cook time has elapsed, leave inside air fryer for 5 minutes before opening. Remove from air fryer and let cool completely, as the granola will crisp up as it cools.

5 Prepare each bowl by stirring together Greek yogurt and mashed berries. Sweeten with honey to taste, if desired.

6 Top the bowl with $1/4$ cup of the granola and your choice of fresh fruits.

7 Granola will stay crisp in an airtight container for up to 3 days.

Mona's Tips

To re-crisp granola, air fry for 3 minutes at 300°F and let cool.

Calories per serving: 305 · Fat: 10.5g · Net Carbs: 28g · Fiber: 5g · Sugars: 14g · Protein: 21g

Everything Bagel Bites

Accessory: 6 silicone baking cups · Active Prep Time: 10 mins · Cook Time: 14 mins · Serves: 6

These delectable bagel bites are made gluten and yeast free with the help of the cultures in Greek yogurt. I add "everything" bagel seasoning both inside and on top for a ton of bagel flavor and bake a dollop of cream cheese in the center for an all-in-one breakfast bite made with minimal effort!

INGREDIENTS

Avocado oil spray

1 large egg

$^1/_3$ cup plain nonfat Greek yogurt

3 tablespoons water, divided

$^1/_2$ cup all-purpose gluten-free flour

1 teaspoon baking powder

2 teaspoons everything bagel seasoning, plus more to top

3 tablespoons reduced-fat cream cheese

Mona's Tips

Want another delicious recipe idea? These bagel bites can also be made with your choice of fruit preserves in place of the cream cheese. Simply omit the everything bagel seasoning or replace with poppyseeds to better complement the fruit.

DIRECTIONS

1 Lightly spray 6 silicone baking cups with avocado oil spray.

2 Separate the egg white into a mixing bowl and egg yolk into a smaller bowl. Set egg yolk aside.

3 To the egg white in the mixing bowl, whisk in Greek yogurt and 2 tablespoons water. Add flour, baking powder, and 2 teaspoons everyting bagel seasoning (for flavor throughout) and fold until combined into a thick batter.

4 Evenly fill the 6 baking cups with the batter and press $^1/_2$ tablespoon of cream cheese into the center of each bagel bite. Place baking cups in the air fryer basket.

325°F air fry 6 mins

5 Whisk 1 tablespoon of water into the reserved egg yolk to create an egg wash and lightly brush over the tops of the egg bites. Sprinkle everything bagel seasoning over the egg wash.

325°F air fry 6–8 mins

6 Bagel bites are done when puffed up and golden brown around the edges. Serve warm. Store refrigerated.

Calories per serving: 85 · Fat: 2g · Net Carbs: 8g · Fiber: 1.5g · Sugars: 1g · Protein: 4g

Avocado Baked Eggs

Active Prep Time: 10 mins · Cook Time: 14 mins · Serves: 2

Whole eggs are cracked right into a halved avocado in this easy recipe that makes a real impact in both flavor and presentation. As you get plenty of creaminess from the warm avocado, I like to serve this topped with fresh pico de gallo, but a sprinkling of Cotija cheese is also great!

INGREDIENTS

1 large Hass avocado

2 small eggs

$^1/_2$ teaspoon Chili Spice Blend (see page 10)

Salt and pepper

$^1/_2$ cup pico de gallo or salsa

1 tablespoon chopped cilantro or parsley

Mona's Tips

There should be enough room in most air fryers to double this recipe with 2 avocados (halved) and 4 eggs. Once doubled, you may need to add an extra 2 minutes to the cook time to ensure the egg whites have set.

DIRECTIONS

1 Cut avocado in half and remove pit. Using a sharp spoon, remove $^1/_3$ of the avocado to make a larger divot to crack the eggs into. This avocado can be mashed and served alongside the finished baked eggs.

2 Crack an egg into each avocado and season with the spice blend, salt, and pepper. Transfer to the air fryer basket.

300°F   air fry   12–14 mins

3 Cook just until the whites of the eggs have set to your liking.

4 Serve each avocado half topped with pico de gallo and chopped cilantro or parsley.

Calories per serving: 220 · Fat: 16.5g · Net Carbs: 7g · Fiber: 5.5g · Sugars: 0.5g · Protein: 6g

Snackertaining

Margherita Pizza Dip

Accessory: 7-inch baking dish · Active Prep Time: 15 mins · Cook Time: 15 mins · Serves: 6

This recipe has everything you want from a classic creamy spinach dip, with the addition of tomatoes and fresh basil that give it a pizza flavor. Plus, the air fryer provides a wonderfully browned top to the dip...So good!

INGREDIENTS

Olive oil spray

8 ounces reduced-fat cream cheese, softened

1 (14.5-ounce) can petite diced tomatoes, with liquid

2 cups frozen chopped spinach, thawed and drained

1/4 cup chopped fresh basil

1 tablespoon minced red onion or shallot

2 teaspoons minced garlic

2 teaspoons balsamic glaze

2 teaspoons Mediterranean Spice Blend (see page 11)

1/2 teaspoon salt

1/4 cup shredded Parmesan cheese

Mona's Tips

I like to air fry dips like this in an oven-safe ceramic serving bowl, as it will hold its heat and keep the dip warm well after cooking.

DIRECTIONS

1 Spray a 7-inch baking dish with olive oil spray.

2 In a mixing bowl, fold together softened cream cheese, diced tomatoes, thawed spinach, basil, onion, garlic, balsamic glaze, spice blend, and salt.

3 Spread the cream cheese mixture in the greased baking dish and top with the shredded Parmesan cheese. Place baking dish in the air fryer basket.

300°F air fry 13–15 mins

4 Dip is done when bubbly-hot around the edges and the Parmesan on top is golden brown. Serve alongside gluten-free crackers or crisp vegetables, for dipping.

Calories per serving: 130 · Fat: 8g · Net Carbs: 7g · Fiber: 2g · Sugars: 5g · Protein: 7g

Savory or Sweet Chickpea Snacks

Active Prep Time: 5 mins · Cook Time: 20 mins · Serves: 4

These crunchy chickpeas make a great low-calorie snack that is packed with protein and can be tossed in a variety of flavors to suit your mood or taste. When making them "Savory," I like to use my Chili Spice Blend, Barbecue Spice Blend, or Mediterranean Spice Blend (see pages 10–11). When making them "Sweet," I keep things simple with cinnamon and a hint of ginger for added depth.

INGREDIENTS

1 (15.5-ounce) can chickpeas (garbanzo beans)

Olive oil spray

Savory Spices

1 1/2 tablespoons any spice blend (see pages 10–11)

1/4 teaspoon salt

Sweet Spices

2 tablespoons light brown sugar

2 teaspoons ground cinnamon

1/2 teaspoon ground ginger

Mona's Tips

Nutritional information for this recipe is based on the Savory preparation. The Sweet preparation has 130 calories per serving, 6g of sugar, and the same amount of fat, fiber, and protein.

DIRECTIONS

1 Drain and rinse chickpeas before transferring to the air fryer basket.

375°F   air fry   5 mins

2 Spray the partially cooked chickpeas with olive oil spray on all sides and continue cooking. Shake basket halfway through the cook time.

375°F   air fry   10–13 mins

3 Cook until chickpeas are crispy and lightly browned.

4 Transfer to a mixing bowl and spray with additional olive oil spray. Toss in 1/2 of the savory or sweet ingredients. Return to the air fryer basket.

375°F   air fry   2 mins

5 Toss in the remaining 1/2 of the savory or sweet ingredients and let cool at least 5 minutes before serving. Store in an airtight container for up to 5 days.

Calories per serving: 110 · Fat: 2g · Net Carbs: 11g · Fiber: 6g · Sugars: 1g · Protein: 5.5g

Orange Chicken Meatballs

Active Prep Time: 20 mins · Cook Time: 14 mins · Serves: 4

Orange chicken, one of the most popular Asian takeout dishes, was my inspiration for these party meatballs made with lean ground chicken breast. It's familiar and satisfying flavors presented in a new and unique way! The orange sauce is also great over shrimp or fish!

INGREDIENTS

Avocado oil spray

Meatballs

1 pound ground chicken breast

1 large egg, beaten

$1/4$ cup gluten-free panko breadcrumbs

2 green onions, minced

$1 1/2$ tablespoons coconut aminos or reduced-sodium tamari soy sauce

1 teaspoon orange zest

2 teaspoons sesame oil

Orange Sauce

$1/2$ cup orange juice

1 tablespoon coconut aminos or reduced-sodium tamari soy sauce

2 teaspoons honey

1 teaspoon orange zest

$1/4$ teaspoon crushed red pepper flakes

$1 1/2$ teaspoons cornstarch

1 tablespoon cold water

1 teaspoon sesame oil

DIRECTIONS

1 Spray the air fryer basket with avocado oil spray.

2 In a mixing bowl, use your hands to combine all meatball ingredients.

3 To keep the ground chicken from sticking to your hands, spray them with avocado oil spray. Form the meatball mixture into golf ball–sized balls and place in the air fryer. Use tongs to flip the meatballs halfway through the cook time.

> **375°F air fry 12–14 mins**

4 Meatballs are done when lightly browned and a meat thermometer registers 165°F.

5 Meanwhile, prepare the orange sauce by placing orange juice in a small saucepan on the stovetop over medium heat. Whisk in coconut aminos, honey, orange zest, and pepper flakes and bring up to a simmer.

6 Whisk cornstarch into 1 tablespoon of cold water and then whisk into the simmering sauce. Stirring constantly, let simmer at least 1 minute.

7 Remove from heat and stir in sesame oil. Toss cooked meatballs in the sauce before serving.

Calories per serving: 230 · Fat: 7g · Net Carbs: 13g · Fiber: 0g · Sugars: 5.5g · Protein: 28.5g

Turkey Bacon–Wrapped Asparagus

Active Prep Time: 15 mins · Cook Time: 12 mins · Serves: 6

When entertaining, finger-food appetizers should be satisfying! This recipe proves that you can create something wholesome your guests will absolutely love. Savory turkey bacon is wrapped around bundles of crisp and nutritious asparagus and then served alongside a quick and easy honey Dijon sauce for dipping.

INGREDIENTS

1 pound thin asparagus, stalks trimmed

1 tablespoon olive oil

1/2 teaspoon garlic powder

1/4 teaspoon salt

1/4 teaspoon pepper

12 strips nitrate-free turkey bacon

Honey Dijon Sauce

1/4 cup nonfat plain Greek yogurt

2 tablespoons Dijon mustard

1 tablespoon honey

DIRECTIONS

1 Toss asparagus in olive oil, garlic powder, salt, and pepper.

2 Tightly wrap a strip of turkey bacon around 3 pieces of asparagus and use a wooden toothpick to secure it in place. Transfer to the air fryer basket and repeat with the remaining asparagus.

> 375°F   air fry   10–12 mins

3 Cook until bacon is browned and asparagus is crisp-tender.

4 Meanwhile, prepare the honey Dijon sauce by stirring together all ingredients. Serve alongside the wrapped asparagus, for dipping.

Mona's Tips

I like to make this with thin asparagus in bundles of 3, but thicker asparagus can be wrapped in bundles of 2 to ensure they cook crisp-tender at the same time the bacon crisps.

Calories per serving: 125 · Fat: 7g · Net Carbs: 4.5g · Fiber: 1.5g · Sugars: 4.5g · Protein: 6.5g

Roasted Peanuts

Active Prep Time: 5 mins · Cook Time: 20 mins · Serves: 8

You are in for an amazing experience! Warm, freshly roasted peanuts have such a rich and delicious flavor. It's like the difference between popping fresh popcorn versus buying a bag from a store! Spice up the shells for added finger-licking flavor, or enjoy them just as they are!

INGREDIENTS

4 cups raw peanuts in the shell

Olive oil spray

Popcorn salt, to taste

Cajun Peanuts

4 cups raw peanuts in the shell

Olive oil spray

1 tablespoon Cajun seasoning

Barbecue Peanuts

4 cups raw peanuts in the shell

Olive oil spray

1 tablespoon Barbecue Spice
  Blend (see page 11)

$1/4$ teaspoon salt

Mona's Tips

The raw peanuts needed for this can usually be found in the produce department, unrefrigerated, in large bags.

DIRECTIONS

1 For plain peanuts, simply place in the air fryer basket.

2 For salted or seasoned peanuts, place in a large mixing bowl and generously spray with olive oil spray. Add seasonings and toss to coat the shells. Transfer to the air fryer basket.

3 Shake peanuts halfway through the cook time. For seasoned peanuts, use a rubber spatula to gently flip the peanuts, as shaking the basket will cause the seasoning to fall off the shells.

325°F   air fry   18–20 mins

4 Peanuts are done when shells are lightly browned and cracking into one gives off the smell of peanut butter, rather than the earthy smell of raw peanuts.

Calories per serving: 155 · Fat: 13.5g · Net Carbs: 1.5g · Fiber: 2.5g · Sugars: 1g · Protein: 7g

Zucchini Chips with Lemon and Herb Dip

Active Prep Time: 20 mins · Cook Time: 12 mins · Serves: 4

Perfect for snacking or entertaining (Snackertaining!), these crispy air fried zucchini rounds are made for dipping. They're amazing dipped into any marinara sauce, but I really love them alongside this lemon and herb dip.

INGREDIENTS

1 large zucchini, sliced 1/4-inch thick

Salt

1 large egg, beaten

1/2 teaspoon garlic powder

1/4 teaspoon pepper

3/4 cup gluten-free
   seasoned breadcrumbs

2 tablespoons grated
   Parmesan cheese

Olive oil spray

Lemon and Herb Dip

1/2 cup nonfat plain Greek yogurt

1 tablespoon milk or
   plant-based milk

1 tablespoon chopped
   fresh oregano

2 teaspoons lemon zest

1 teaspoon minced garlic

1 teaspoon honey

1/2 teaspoon dried dill

Salt and pepper, to taste

DIRECTIONS

1 Place sliced zucchini on paper towels, lightly season with salt, and let rest 5 minutes to remove any excess liquid.

2 In a wide bowl, whisk together egg, garlic powder, pepper, and a pinch of salt.

3 In a separate wide bowl, stir together breadcrumbs and Parmesan cheese.

4 Dip the zucchini slices in the egg mixture before coating with the breadcrumbs on both sides. Continue until all are breaded.

5 Spray the breaded zucchini with olive oil spray on both sides. Place in the air fryer basket in as close to a single layer as possible. It is okay to overlap a few. Use tongs to flip halfway through the cook time.

> **400°F air fry 10–12 mins**

6 Meanwhile, prepare the lemon and herb dip by stirring together all ingredients. Season with salt and pepper to taste. Serve alongside the cooked zucchini chips.

Calories per serving: 130 · Fat: 3.5g · Net Carbs: 16g · Fiber: 1g · Sugars: 4g · Protein: 8.5g

Pineapple Ginger Chicken Wings

Active Prep Time: 15 mins · Cook Time: 18 mins · Serves: 8

These crispy (without any breading!) air fried wings are tossed in a tangy and slightly sweet glaze made from puréed pineapple and ginger.

INGREDIENTS

Avocado oil spray

2 pounds split chicken wings

Salt, pepper, and ground ginger

Pineapple Ginger Glaze

$1/2$ cup canned pineapple in 100% juice, juice reserved

$1\,1/2$ tablespoons coconut aminos or reduced-sodium tamari soy sauce

$1\,1/2$ tablespoons ginger paste

1 teaspoon minced garlic

$1/4$ teaspoon crushed red pepper flakes

Honey, optional

DIRECTIONS

1 Spray air fryer basket with avocado oil spray. Season wings with salt, pepper, and ground ginger and place in the air fryer basket. Use tongs to flip wings halfway through cook time.

> **400°F · air fry · 12 mins**

2 Meanwhile, prepare the glaze by placing pineapple, aminos, ginger, and garlic in a food processor. Add 1 tablespoon of pineapple juice or as much as needed to process until smooth. Stir in red pepper flakes. If you prefer a sweeter glaze, sweeten with honey to taste.

3 Transfer $1/3$ of the glaze to a separate bowl (to prevent cross-contamination) and brush that on the tops of the wings before air frying a few minutes longer, or until the internal temperature of the thickest wing reaches 165°F.

> **400°F · air fry · 4–6 mins**

4 Toss cooked wings in the remaining $2/3$ of the glaze before serving.

Calories per serving: 235 · Fat: 17g · Net Carbs: 2g · Fiber: 0g · Sugars: 2g · Protein: 17.5g

Nashville Hot Chicken Wings

Active Prep Time: 10 mins · Cook Time: 18 mins · Serves: 8

If you like things HOT, these wings pack a punch that is perfectly offset with a slight tang from a dash of pickle juice and a bit of sweetness from brown sugar.

INGREDIENTS

Avocado oil spray

2 pounds split chicken wings

Salt, pepper, chili powder,
   and cayenne pepper

Nashville Hot Sauce

2 tablespoons Louisiana hot sauce

1 tablespoon butter, melted

1 tablespoon water

2 teaspoons light brown sugar

1 teaspoon pickle juice

$1/4$ teaspoon garlic powder

Mona's Tips

For the crispiest wings in the air fryer, pat dry with paper towels and sprinkle with $1/2$ teaspoon of baking powder before you season. The baking powder promotes browning in chicken skin.

DIRECTIONS

1 Spray air fryer basket with avocado oil spray. Lightly season wings with salt, pepper, chili powder, and cayenne pepper and place in the air fryer basket. Use tongs to flip wings halfway through cook time.

400°F   air fry   16–18 mins

2 Wings are done when the internal temperature of the thickest wing reaches 165°F.

3 Meanwhile, in a large mixing bowl, whisk together all Nashville hot sauce ingredients. Toss the cooked wings in the sauce before serving.

Calories per serving: 240 · Fat: 18.5g · Net Carbs: 1.5g · Fiber: 0g · Sugars: 1g · Protein: 17.5g

Loaded Sweet Potato Waffle Fries

Active Prep Time: 5 mins · Cook Time: 24 mins · Serves: 4

Frozen waffle-cut sweet potato fries are all dressed up in this easy-prep appetizer (or side dish!) that combines the naturally sweet and savory flavors. Topped with crispy turkey bacon, creamy Gorgonzola cheese, and fresh green onions, this is an indulgence that won't weigh you down as traditional (and deep-fried) bacon-cheese fries would.

INGREDIENTS

Avocado oil spray

3 strips nitrate-free turkey bacon

10 ounces frozen waffle-cut sweet potato fries

$^1/_4$ cup crumbled Gorgonzola cheese

2 green onions, sliced

Mona's Tips

I like the contrast of the cool crumbled Gorgonzola with the hot fries; however, you can melt the Gorgonzola onto the fries by adding it in the last 2 minutes of the cook time.

DIRECTIONS

1 Lightly spray the air fryer basket with avocado oil spray and arrange turkey bacon strips in a single layer inside.

375°F air fry 10 mins

2 Cook turkey bacon just until crisp. Remove bacon from air fryer, chop, and set aside.

3 Place frozen sweet potato fries in the air fryer basket. Shake the basket halfway through the cook time.

375°F air fry 12–14 mins

4 Cook fries until crisp. Serve topped with the chopped bacon, crumbled Gorgonzola cheese, and sliced green onion.

Calories per serving: 180 · Fat: 9g · Net Carbs: 18g · Fiber: 3g · Sugars: 4g · Protein: 5g

Mini Black Bean Tostadas

Active Prep Time: 10 mins · Cook Time: 8 mins · Serves: 4

Crispy corn tortillas are topped with black beans, cheese, and pico de gallo in these mini Tex-Mex tostadas that are perfect for entertaining. I like to prep a full sheet pan at once and air fry them as needed!

INGREDIENTS

1/4 cup canned black beans, drained and rinsed

1/4 cup shredded Cheddar Jack cheese

3 tablespoons pico de gallo

1/4 teaspoon chili powder

1/4 teaspoon cumin

1/4 teaspoon salt

4 mini "street taco" corn tortillas

Olive oil spray

Nonfat plain Greek yogurt, to top, optional

Mona's Tips

This recipe can be easily doubled or tripled to feed a crowd. For smaller air fryers, simply cook in batches of 4.

DIRECTIONS

1 In a mixing bowl, fold together black beans, shredded cheese, pico de gallo, chili powder, cumin, and salt.

2 Lay out 4 street taco tortillas, lightly spray with olive oil spray, flip, and then spray the opposite side.

3 Place an equal amount of the black bean and cheese mixture over top each tortilla.

4 Transfer to the air fryer basket in a single layer.

375°F air fry 6–8 mins

5 Tostadas are done when the edges are crisp and golden brown. Serve garnished with a dollop of Greek yogurt, if desired.

Calories per serving: 85 · Fat: 3.5g · Net Carbs: 8g · Fiber: 2g · Sugars: 0.5g · Protein: 3.5g

Potato Latkes

Active Prep Time: 20 mins · Cook Time: 14 mins · Serves: 4

Latkes are one of my famiy favorites, served not only at Chanukah, but for any fun gatherings. Typically, these crispy potato pancakes are fried in a skillet, but using the air fryer packs in the same flavor and crispness! I love to serve them with a dollop of apple sauce or nonfat plain Greek yogurt with green onions or chives.

INGREDIENTS

1 packed cup peeled and grated potato

¼ cup grated onion

½ teaspoon salt

2 tablespoons gluten-free all-purpose flour

1 large egg yolk, beaten

Olive oil spray

Nonfat plain Greek yogurt or unsweetened applesauce, to top, optional

Mona's Tips

This recipe can be easily doubled or tripled to feed a crowd. For smaller air fryers, simply cook in batches of 4.

DIRECTIONS

1 Grate potato and onion with a box grater or food processor's grating blade, measure, and then place over paper towels. Toss with salt and let sit 5 minutes to drain excess liquid. After 5 minutes, press with additional paper towels to remove more liquid.

2 Transfer drained potatoes and onions to a mixing bowl and toss with the flour. Fold in beaten egg yolk to create a loose dough.

3 Spray air fryer basket with olive oil spray. Press the dough into 4 cakes and place in the air fryer basket. Spray the tops with olive oil spray. Cook without flipping.

375°F air fry 12–14 mins

4 Latkes are done when crispy and golden brown. Serve topped with plain Greek yogurt or applesauce, if desired.

Calories per serving: 80 · Fat: 2.5g · Net Carbs: 10.5g · Fiber: 1.5g · Sugars: 1g · Protein: 2g

Asian Edamame Snack Mix

Active Prep Time: 10 mins · Cook Time: 19 mins · Serves: 8

This snack mix is packed with my favorite savory Asian flavors of ginger and sesame. Not only is it unique, but it's lower in fat and added sugar, and higher in protein than anything store-bought. The combination of textures makes this mix so special!

INGREDIENTS

1 cup frozen (out of the shell) edamame

3 cups rice squares cereal

2 cups gluten-free pretzels

$1/2$ cup raw cashews

2 tablespoons sesame oil

2 tablespoons water

1 tablespoon coconut aminos or reduced-sodium tamari soy sauce

1 tablespoon ginger paste

1 teaspoon onion powder

$1/2$ teaspoon garlic powder

Mona's Tips

Want to make the crunchy edamame as its own snack? Simply follow the first step of the recipe and then air fry the edamame alone for 14–15 minutes.

DIRECTIONS

1 Place frozen edamame in the air fryer basket. Shake basket halfway through cook time.

> **325°F   air fry   12 mins**

2 Place cooked edamame, rice squares, pretzels, and cashews in a large mixing bowl.

3 In a small mixing bowl, whisk together sesame oil, water, coconut aminos, ginger paste, and onion and garlic powders.

4 Slowly drizzle the liquid seasoning mixture over the dry ingredients in the large mixing bowl, tossing to evenly coat.

5 Transfer to the air fryer basket. Reduce cooking temperature and shake basket halfway through cook time.

> **275°F   air fry   5–7 mins**

6 Cook just until the rice squares are golden brown and fragrant. Check frequently, as rice squares will brown quickly after 5 minutes. Snack mix will crisp up further as it cools. Store in an airtight container for up to 5 days.

Calories per serving: 195 · Fat: 8g · Net Carbs: 22.5g · Fiber: 2g · Sugars: 3g · Protein: 6g

Buffalo Cauliflower Bites with Blue Cheese Dressing

Active Prep Time: 15 mins · Cook Time: 12 mins · Serves: 4

I love using veggies to create nutritious comfort food snacks. This recipe really takes that to the next level by coating cauliflower florets with buffalo sauce and just a bit of gluten-free breadcrumbs to add a satisfying crunch. They're not chicken wings, but they satisfy that same craving in a far, far healthier way. Just be sure to take them for a dip in my homemade blue cheese dressing!

INGREDIENTS

1 small head cauliflower, chopped into bite-sized pieces

1/4 cup gluten-free breadcrumbs

3 tablespoons buffalo sauce

2 tablespoons butter

1/2 teaspoon garlic powder

Blue Cheese Dressing

1/2 cup nonfat plain Greek yogurt

1/2 cup blue cheese crumbles

1 tablespoon milk or plant-based milk

1/2 teaspoon Worcestershire sauce

1/4 teaspoon garlic powder

1/4 teaspoon salt

1/4 teaspoon pepper

DIRECTIONS

1 In a large mixing bowl, toss chopped cauliflower in breadcrumbs, buffalo sauce, butter, and garlic powder until evenly coated.

2 Transfer to the air fryer basket and cook until cauliflower is crisp-tender and beginning to brown.

400°F   air fry   10–12 mins

3 Meanwhile, prepare the blue cheese dressing by stirring together all ingredients. Serve alongside the cauliflower bites, for dipping.

Mona's Tips

Look for buffalo sauce that has 0g of fat, as some brands are more similar to a dressing than a hot sauce. For more heat, toss the cooked cauliflower in additional buffalo sauce as soon as you remove it from the air fryer.

Calories per serving: 190 · Fat: 10.5g · Net Carbs: 8.5g · Fiber: 4.5g · Sugars: 4g · Protein: 9.5g

Fantastic Falafel with Tahini Sauce

Active Prep Time: 15 mins · Cook Time: 14 mins · Serves: 4

After I came back from an amazingly delicious trip to Israel, I wanted to recreate the (typically fried) falafel I ate there in a healthy but delicious way. With the use of my air fryer, I was able to do it! These round balls are made from chickpeas, parsley, garlic, and aromatic spices before being air fried until golden brown. I like to serve them with a traditional tahini (ground sesame seeds) sauce for dipping!

INGREDIENTS

1 (15.5-ounce) can chickpeas
   (garbanzo beans),
   drained and rinsed

$2/3$ cup packed fresh parsley leaves

$1/4$ cup minced yellow onion

2 tablespoons gluten-free
   all-purpose flour

1 tablespoon minced garlic

1 tablespoon extra-virgin olive oil

2 teaspoons lemon juice

1 teaspoon ground cumin

$1/2$ teaspoon ground coriander

$1/4$ teaspoon salt

Olive oil spray

Tahini Sauce

3 tablespoons unsweetened
   almond milk

2 tablespoons tahini paste

1 teaspoon minced garlic

$1/2$ teaspoon lemon zest

$1/4$ teaspoon ground cumin

DIRECTIONS

1 In a food processor, pulse chickpeas, parsley, onion, flour, garlic, olive oil, lemon juice, cumin, coriander, and salt, just until combined into a crumbly dough.

2 Using your hands, roll the dough into ping pong–sized balls.

3 Spray falafel on all sides with olive oil spray and transfer to the air fryer basket. Shake basket twice as the falafel cooks.

400°F   air fry   12–14 mins

4 Falafel is done when lightly browned and steaming hot in the center.

5 Meanwhile, prepare the tahini sauce by stirring together all ingredients. Serve alongside the cooked falafel, for dipping. Tahini sauce is also great for dipping fresh vegetables!

Mona's Tips

Create falafel wraps with gluten-free pitas, cauliflower pitas, or almond flour tortillas!

Calories per serving: 190 · Fat: 10.5g · Net Carbs: 8.5g · Fiber: 4.5g · Sugars: 4g · Protein: 9.5g

Avocado Fries with Enchilada Dipping Sauce

Active Prep Time: 15 mins · Cook Time: 8 mins · Serves: 6

Creamy avocado is seasoned, breaded, and air fried to crispy perfection in this Tex-Mex appetizer. The combination of the creamy avocado and the spicy, crispy, and satisfying breading makes a healthy-delicious snack!

INGREDIENTS

2 Hass avocados,
   peeled and pitted

Juice of 1 lime

2 large egg whites

1 tablespoon Chili Spice Blend
   (see page 10), divided

$1/2$ teaspoon salt, divided

1 cup gluten-free breadcrumbs

Olive oil spray

Enchilada Dipping Sauce

$1/4$ cup nonfat plain Greek yogurt

$1/4$ cup red enchilada sauce

$1/2$ teaspoon onion powder

Salt, to taste

Mona's Tips

For the best browning, lightly spray the avocado with additional olive oil spray after flipping halfway through the cook time.

DIRECTIONS

1 Slice avocados into $1/2$-inch wedges and drizzle with lime juice to prevent browning.

2 In a wide bowl, whisk together egg whites, $1/2$ tablespoon of the spice blend, and $1/4$ teaspoon of the salt.

3 In a separate wide bowl, stir together breadcrumbs, $1/2$ tablespoon of the spice blend, and the remaining $1/4$ teaspoon of salt.

4 Dip the avocado wedges in the egg white mixture before coating with the breadcrumbs on both sides. Continue until all are breaded.

5 Spray the breaded avocado with olive oil spray on both sides. Place in the air fryer basket in a single layer. You will most likely need to cook in 2 batches. Flip each batch halfway through the cook time.

400°F air fry 6–8 mins

6 Meanwhile, prepare the enchilada dipping sauce by stirring together all ingredients and seasoning with salt to taste. Serve alongside the fried avocado, for dipping.

Calories per serving: 150 · Fat: 8g · Net Carbs: 13g · Fiber: 3.5g · Sugars: 1g · Protein: 3.5g

Crab Cakes with Remoulade Sauce

Active Prep Time: 15 mins · Cook Time: 12 mins · Serves: 4

While you can make these crab cakes with 6 ounces of fresh crab meat if you'd like, canned lump crab meat is far easier, more cost-conscious, and available to purchase any time of the year. Packing the rest of the cake with bright and fresh flavors makes these a restaurant-quality appetizer that is full of protein!

INGREDIENTS

1 large egg white

$1/4$ cup gluten-free panko breadcrumbs

1 tablespoon chopped fresh parsley

2 teaspoons whole-grain mustard

$1/2$ teaspoon paprika

$1/2$ teaspoon lemon zest

$1/4$ teaspoon onion powder

$1/4$ teaspoon pepper

6 ounces lump crab meat, drained

2 tablespoons finely diced bell pepper

Olive oil spray

Remoulade Sauce

$1/4$ cup nonfat plain Greek yogurt

1 tablespoon capers, minced

1 teaspoon Dijon mustard

$1/2$ teaspoon prepared horseradish

$1/2$ teaspoon minced garlic

$1/2$ teaspoon paprika

DIRECTIONS

1 In a mixing bowl, whisk egg white. Fold in breadcrumbs, parsley, mustard, paprika, lemon zest, onion powder, and pepper.

2 Gently fold in crab meat and diced bell pepper. Cover and refrigerate for 30 minutes.

3 Meanwhile, prepare the remoulade sauce by stirring together all ingredients. Cover and refrigerate until ready to serve.

4 Form the chilled crab mixture into 4 cakes. Spray the air fryer basket and both sides of the crab cakes with olive oil spray. Place the crab cakes in the air fryer basket.

375°F   air fry   10–12 mins

5 Crab cakes are done when lightly browned and slightly springy to the touch. Serve alongside the prepared remoulade sauce.

Calories per serving: 85 · Fat: 1.5g · Net Carbs: 6g · Fiber: 0.5g · Sugars: 1g · Protein: 12g

Complete Meals

Balsamic Salmon with Sweet Potatoes and Sprouts

Active Prep Time: 10 mins · Cook Time: 26 mins · Serves: 2

Whenever I make this dish for dinner, it gets rave reviews, and I am often told it is BETTER than any seafood dish at a fancy restaurant! The special glaze simply makes this dish—a savory and sweet combination of balsamic vinegar, rosemary, orange zest, and honey.

INGREDIENTS

1 $1/2$ tablespoons olive oil

1 tablespoon balsamic vinegar

1 tablespoon honey

1 teaspoon orange zest

$1/2$ teaspoon dried rosemary

$1/4$ teaspoon salt

$1/4$ teaspoon pepper

3 cups Brussels sprouts, halved

2 cups chopped sweet potato

$1/2$ medium red bell pepper, chopped

2 fresh wild salmon fillets (about 5 ounces each)

Mona's Tips

Be sure to cut the sweet potatoes into small (around $1/2$-inch) cubes to ensure that they cook in the same amount of time as the other vegetables.

DIRECTIONS

1 In a mixing bowl, whisk together olive oil, balsamic vinegar, honey, orange zest, rosemary, salt, and pepper. Set aside half of this mixture in a separate container to later coat the salmon.

2 Add the Brussels sprouts, sweet potato, and bell pepper to the other half of the olive oil mixture and toss to coat. Transfer vegetables to the air fryer basket.

400°F   air fry   12 mins

3 Shake vegetables in the basket.

4 Flip salmon fillets in the reserved olive oil and balsamic mixture to coat. Place over top the partially cooked vegetables.

400°F   air fry   12–14 mins

5 Cook until sweet potatoes are fork-tender and salmon easily flakes with a fork.

Calories per serving: 465 · Fat: 15g · Net Carbs: 51g · Fiber: 9.5g · Sugars: 18g · Protein: 35g

Bruschetta Chicken with Eggplant

Accessory: metal rack · Active Prep Time: 20 mins · Cook Time: 20 mins · Serves: 2

This lighter, fresher take on chicken Parmesan replaces marinara sauce with a freshly chopped tomato bruschetta that enhances the crispiness of the breaded chicken. Air-roasted eggplant is cooked right along with the chicken for even more Mediterranean flavors.

INGREDIENTS

1 small eggplant

2 teaspoons olive oil

2 teaspoons Mediterranean Spice Blend (see page 11), divided

Salt and pepper

1 large egg, beaten

$1/2$ cup gluten-free panko breadcrumbs

2 tablespoons grated Parmesan cheese

2 (6-ounce) boneless, skinless chicken breast fillets

Olive oil spray

3 cups zucchini noodles, steamed

Bruschetta

2 small Roma tomatoes, diced

1 tablespoon chopped fresh basil

2 cloves garlic, minced

1 teaspoon balsamic vinegar

1 teaspoon olive oil

DIRECTIONS

1 Trim ends from eggplant and discard. Chop eggplant into 1-inch cubes. Transfer to a mixing bowl.

2 Add olive oil, 1 teaspoon of the spice blend, $1/4$ teaspoon of salt, and $1/4$ teaspoon of pepper to the eggplant and toss to coat. Transfer to the air fryer basket.

3 In a wide bowl, whisk together egg, the remaining spice blend, and a pinch of salt and pepper. In a separate wide bowl, stir together breadcrumbs and Parmesan cheese.

4 Dip the chicken breasts in the egg and then press into the breadcrumb mix on both sides to coat. Spray breaded chicken with olive oil spray on both sides.

5 If you have room, place chicken beside the eggplant. Otherwise, place chicken atop a metal rack over the eggplant. Shake eggplant and flip chicken halfway through the cook time.

350°F   air fry   18–20 mins

6 Chicken is done when a meat thermometer inserted into the thickest part registers 165°F.

7 Meanwhile, prepare the bruschetta by folding together all ingredients. Serve over cooked chicken alongside steamed zucchini noodles.

Calories per serving: 495 · Fat: 14g · Net Carbs: 33.5g · Fiber: 10g · Sugars: 8g · Protein: 51g

Hoisin Pork Tenderloin with Vegetables

Active Prep Time: 10 mins · Cook Time: 22 mins · Serves: 4

Lean pork tenderloin is glazed with sweet and savory hoisin sauce in this complete Asian meal with broccoli, carrots, and brown rice.

INGREDIENTS

2 cups baby carrots

$1 \frac{1}{2}$ tablespoons sesame oil, divided

2 teaspoons coconut aminos or reduced-sodium tamari soy sauce

$\frac{1}{2}$ teaspoon ground ginger

$\frac{1}{4}$ teaspoon onion powder

$\frac{1}{4}$ teaspoon pepper

1 (1.25-pound) pork tenderloin

1 pound broccoli florets

$\frac{1}{4}$ teaspoon garlic powder

3 tablespoons gluten-free hoisin sauce, divided

2 cups cooked brown rice

1 teaspoon toasted sesame seeds, optional

Mona's Tips

Hoisin sauce is a sweet Asian barbecue sauce. Traditional hoisin contains a small amount of wheat, but gluten-free hoisin is available. In a pinch, gluten-free teriyaki marinade can be substituted.

DIRECTIONS

1 In a mixing bowl, toss carrots with $\frac{1}{2}$ tablespoon of sesame oil and transfer to the air fryer basket.

2 In a small mixing bowl, whisk together $\frac{1}{2}$ tablespoon of sesame oil, aminos, ginger, onion powder, and pepper. Drizzle over the pork and roll to lightly coat on all sides. Place over the carrots in the air fryer basket. Note: For smaller air fryers, cut tenderloin into 2 shorter halves to better fit.

400°F   air fry   8 mins

3 Toss broccoli with garlic powder and the last $\frac{1}{2}$ tablespoon of sesame oil. Arrange around pork in the air fryer.

400°F   air fry   8 mins

4 Flip pork and shake the vegetables in the basket. Brush the top of the pork with 2 tablespoons of the hoisin sauce.

400°F   air fry   4–6 mins

5 Pork is done when a meat thermometer inserted into the center registers 145°F for medium or 150°F for medium-well.

6 Toss the cooked broccoli and carrots in the remaining tablespoon of hoisin sauce before serving alongside the sliced pork and cooked brown rice. Top with toasted sesame seeds, if desired.

Calories per serving: 405 · Fat: 11g · Net Carbs: 35.5g · Fiber: 7g · Sugars: 9g · Protein: 35g

Very Veggie Quinoa Bowls

Active Prep Time: 20 mins · Cook Time: 16 mins · Serves: 2

I am always looking for ways to cook and eat more "plant-forward" while being mindful of packing vegetables and whole grains into my meals. In this bowl, protein-packed quinoa is topped with an assortment of colorful vegetables that are "roasted" right in the air fryer. Pepitas are sprinkled over the top for a bit of crunch, and balsamic glaze adds just a bit of acid and sweetness. It's a meal packed with nutrients and fiber!

INGREDIENTS

2 carrots, chopped

1 1/2 cups broccoli florets

1 1/2 cups cauliflower florets

1 cup baby bella mushrooms, halved

1 medium red bell pepper, seeded and chopped large

1 tablespoon olive oil

1 tablespoon Roasting Spice Blend (see page 10)

1/4 teaspoon salt

1/4 teaspoon pepper

1 1/2 cups cooked quinoa

2 tablespoons roasted pepitas (shelled pumpkin seeds)

2 tablespoons balsamic glaze

DIRECTIONS

1 In a mixing bowl, toss together carrots, broccoli, cauliflower, mushrooms, bell pepper, olive oil, spice blend, salt, and pepper.

2 Transfer to the air fryer basket. Shake basket halfway through the cook time.

400°F air fry 14–16 mins

3 Vegetables are done when carrots are crisp-tender.

4 Arrange bowls by filling with an equal amount of cooked quinoa and topping with an equal amount of the cooked vegetables. Sprinkle with pepitas and drizzle with balsamic glaze before serving.

Mona's Tips

Pepitas (a variety of pumpkin seed that naturally has no hull/shell) can usually be found in the produce section near other seeds and nuts.

Calories per serving: 430 · Fat: 14.5g · Net Carbs: 50g · Fiber: 13g · Sugars: 15.5g · Protein: 16g

Shrimp Scampi with Italian Vegetables

Active Prep Time: 10 mins · Cook Time: 10 mins · Serves: 2

This "toss and go" recipe has shrimp, squash, zucchini, and tomatoes that are all air fried together for maximum simplicity and absolutely amazing flavor. The secret to achieving a ton of flavor is seasoning first, but then tossing the cooked shrimp and vegetables in butter, lemon, and garlic AFTER cooking to boost things up!

INGREDIENTS

8 ounces large uncooked
   shrimp, peeled

1 large yellow squash, sliced

1 zucchini, sliced

1 cup grape tomatoes

2 teaspoons olive oil

$1/4$ teaspoon each: oregano,
   garlic powder, salt, and pepper

1 tablespoon butter, melted

Juice of $1/2$ lemon

2 tablespoons chopped
   fresh parsley

2 teaspoons minced garlic

Pinch crushed red pepper flakes

4 ounces gluten-free pasta, cooked

DIRECTIONS

1 In a mixing bowl, toss together shrimp, squash, zucchini, grape tomatoes, olive oil, oregano, garlic powder, salt, and pepper.

2 Transfer to the air fryer basket and arrange tomatoes on top. Shake basket halfway through the cook time.

> **400°F   air fry   8–10 mins**

3 Shrimp are done when opaque throughout.

4 In a mixing bowl, whisk together melted butter, lemon juice, parsley, garlic, and red pepper flakes. Add the cooked shrimp and vegetables and toss to coat.

5 Serve over pasta cooked according to the package directions and seasoned with salt and pepper to taste.

> **Mona's Tips**

This can also be made with frozen shrimp by air frying the shrimp for 3 minutes at 400°F to slightly thaw before tossing with the uncooked vegetables in the first step.

Calories per serving: 460 · Fat: 14.5g · Net Carbs: 43.5g · Fiber: 11.5g · Sugars: 9.5g · Protein: 35.5g

Buttermilk Chicken and Fries Platter

Active Prep Time: 15 mins · Cook Time: 28 mins · Serves: 2

I love using my air fryer to make a comforting "fried chicken" dinner of crispy buttermilk-marinated tenders with sweet potato fries and homemade coleslaw.

INGREDIENTS

3/4 cup low-fat buttermilk

1 tablespoon gluten-free 1-to-1 flour

1/2 teaspoon hot pepper sauce

1/4 teaspoon each: salt, pepper, paprika, and garlic powder

12 ounces chicken tenderloins

1 large sweet potato, cut into fries

2 teaspoons cornstarch

Olive oil spray

1 cup gluten-free breadcrumbs

1/2 teaspoon smoked paprika

Coleslaw

8 ounces shredded coleslaw cabbage mix

2 tablespoons nonfat plain Greek yogurt

2 tablespoons almond milk

1 tablespoon cider vinegar

2 teaspoons light brown sugar

1 teaspoon Dijon mustard

1/4 teaspoon celery salt

Pinch pepper

DIRECTIONS

1 In a mixing bowl, whisk together buttermilk, flour, hot sauce, salt, pepper, paprika, and garlic powder. Add chicken tenderloins to the mixture, cover, and refrigerate 1 hour before preparing. Soak the sweet potatoes in cold water for the same hour.

2 Drain and pat sweet potatoes dry, sprinkle with cornstarch, spray with olive oil spray, and transfer to the air fryer basket. Shake basket halfway through the cook time.

400°F air fry 13 mins

3 Remove fries and transfer to a plate. Set aside. Remove chicken from the buttermilk before pressing into the breadcrumbs on both sides. Spray with olive oil spray on both sides and transfer to the empty air fryer basket. Flip halfway through the cook time.

400°F air fry 10 mins

4 Season the partially cooked sweet potato fries with smoked paprika and place over the chicken tenders in the basket for a final round of cooking.

400°F air fry 3–5 mins

5 Meanwhile, prepare the coleslaw by folding together all ingredients. Serve alongside the rest of the meal.

Calories per serving: 455 · Fat: 8.5g · Net Carbs: 47.5g · Fiber: 8.5g · Sugars: 14g · Protein: 40g

Smoked Pork Chops with Apples and Butternut Squash

Active Prep Time: 20 mins · Cook Time: 22 mins · Serves: 2

Smoked pork chops are an often-overlooked protein that is usually sold near the ham in the grocery store. They're lean, fully cooked, and perfectly complemented by the butternut squash and apples in this full meal. The onion gravy (included in the nutritional information) is optional but really ties everything together. If you don't eat pork, this same meal can be prepared with 4 links of precooked chicken sausage in the same cook time.

INGREDIENTS

3 cups cubed butternut squash

1/2 teaspoon dried thyme

1/4 teaspoon ground cinnamon

1/4 teaspoon salt

1/4 teaspoon pepper

2 teaspoons olive oil, divided

1 apple, cored and cut into wedges

4 boneless smoked pork chops

Olive oil spray

Onion Gravy

1/2 cup diced yellow onion

1/2 tablespoon butter

1/3 cup chicken stock

2 teaspoons chopped sage

1 1/2 teaspoons cornstarch

1 tablespoon cold water

Salt and pepper

DIRECTIONS

1 In a mixing bowl, toss the cubed butternut squash in thyme, cinnamon, salt, pepper, and 1 teaspoon of the olive oil. Transfer to the air fryer basket.

400°F air fry 10 mins

2 Shake basket. Toss apple wedges in the remaining teaspoon of olive oil and place over top the squash.

400°F air fry 6 mins

3 Shake basket. Place smoked pork chops over the squash and apples and spray with olive oil spray. Cook just until pork is heated through and beginning to crisp around the edges.

400°F air fry 4–6 mins

4 Meanwhile, prepare the onion gravy by placing onions and butter in a small saucepan on the stovetop over medium heat. Stirring occasionally, let cook 10 minutes to brown onions.

5 Add chicken stock and sage to the saucepan and bring up to a simmer. Whisk cornstarch into 1 tablespoon of cold water and then whisk into the gravy. Stirring constantly, let simmer at least 1 minute. Season with salt and pepper to taste before serving over pork chops.

Calories per serving: 420 · Fat: 15g · Net Carbs: 28g · Fiber: 7g · Sugars: 17g · Protein: 33g

Quinoa Stuffed Peppers

Active Prep Time: 15 mins · Cook Time: 12 mins · Serves: 2

This light (and vegan) meal is fully served inside air-roasted peppers. The fulfilling filling is made easy with cooked quinoa (I buy mine in precooked pouches near the cooked rice), black beans, frozen corn kernels, and salsa. The best part of the meal? I LOVE how the quinoa gets toasty and crisp after cooking, combined with the creamy texture of the guacamole on top!

INGREDIENTS

2 medium bell peppers

1 cup cooked quinoa

$^3/_4$ cup canned black beans, drained and rinsed

$^1/_3$ cup frozen corn kernels, thawed

$^1/_4$ cup salsa

1 teaspoon Chili Spice Blend (see page 10)

$^1/_4$ teaspoon onion powder

$^1/_4$ teaspoon salt

Olive oil spray

$^1/_4$ cup guacamole

Mona's Tips

I like to make these stuffed peppers with the pepper cooked on the outside and still fresh and crisp on the inside. For fully cooked peppers inside and out, air fry the halved peppers for 4 minutes before stuffing with the filling to finish cooking.

DIRECTIONS

1 Cut peppers in half lengthwise and remove cores and seeds to make each into 2 pepper bowls to be stuffed.

2 In a mixing bowl, fold together quinoa, black beans, corn, salsa, spice blend, onion powder, and salt to make the filling.

3 Spoon an equal amount of the filling into each pepper half.

4 Lightly spray the air fryer basket with olive oil spray, place the peppers inside, and then lightly spray the sides and tops of the peppers.

350°F   air fry   10–12 mins

5 Cook until peppers are tender on the outside and the quinoa on the top is crisp. Serve 2 stuffed pepper halves per serving, each topped with a dollop of guacamole.

Calories per serving: 305 · Fat: 8g · Net Carbs: 40g · Fiber: 11.5g · Sugars: 8g · Protein: 12g

Hummus Chicken with Pistachio Gremolata

Accessory: metal rack · Active Prep Time: 15 mins · Cook Time: 17 mins · Serves: 2

This yummy meal was inspired by my nephew Zach, and then passed on to me by my sisters Laurey and Vickie! I just love it! By cooking this in the air fryer, the hummus creates a beautiful crust on the outside, yet stays creamy on the inside. I got creative with the veggies by adding green beans and artichoke hearts, plus a nutty pistachio gremolata topping that makes this meal extra special!

INGREDIENTS

1 (14-ounce) can or jar baby artichoke hearts, drained

8 ounces green beans, ends trimmed

2 teaspoons olive oil, divided

Salt, pepper, and garlic powder

2 (6-ounce) boneless, skinless chicken breast fillets

Juice of $1/2$ lemon

Oregano, dried dill, and cumin

$1/4$ cup hummus

Pistachio Gremolata

2 tablespoons minced pistachios

2 tablespoons minced sundried tomato

2 tablespoons minced fresh parsley

2 teaspoons minced garlic

Zest of $1/2$ lemon

1 teaspoon olive oil

$1/4$ teaspoon pepper

DIRECTIONS

1 In a mixing bowl, toss artichoke hearts and green beans in 1 teaspoon of the olive oil and $1/4$ teaspoon each of salt, pepper, and garlic powder. Transfer to the air fryer basket.

2 Drizzle lemon juice over chicken breasts and rub with the remaining teaspoon olive oil. Lightly season on both sides with salt, pepper, garlic powder, oregano, dried dill, and cumin.

3 Spread 2 tablespoons of hummus over top each seasoned chicken breast.

4 If you have room, place chicken beside the vegetables in the air fryer. Otherwise, place atop a metal rack over the vegetables.

375°F   air fry   15–17 mins

5 Chicken is done when a meat thermometer inserted into the thickest part registers 165°F.

6 Meanwhile, prepare the pistachio gremolata by combining all ingredients. Serve over top the chicken, green beans, and artichokes.

Calories per serving: 475 · Fat: 17g · Net Carbs: 18g · Fiber: 13.5g · Sugars: 7.5g · Protein: 50g

Curry Tofu Bowls with Spicy Peanut Sauce

Accessory: metal rack · Active Prep Time: 20 mins · Cook Time: 20 mins · Serves: 2

I feel the air fryer was made to cook tofu, and it comes out so well, especially when you use it to top a wholesome bowl like this. The peanut sauce is amazing, and it really makes the meal!

INGREDIENTS

12 ounces extra-firm tofu

1 tablespoon cornstarch

1 tablespoon curry powder

Salt and pepper

Avocado oil spray

8 ounces broccoli florets

4 ounces baby bella mushrooms, halved

$1/2$ red bell pepper, chopped

Juice of $1/2$ lemon

$1/2$ teaspoon onion powder

1 cup cooked brown rice

Spicy Peanut Sauce

1 tablespoon natural peanut butter

1 tablespoon coconut aminos or reduced-sodium tamari soy sauce

1 teaspoon sesame oil

1 teaspoon ginger paste

1 teaspoon rice wine vinegar

$1/4$ teaspoon crushed red pepper flakes

DIRECTIONS

1 Press tofu between paper towels to remove excess water. Cut into 1-inch cubes and pat with additional paper towels.

2 Sprinkle tofu with cornstarch and curry powder on at least 2 sides. Lightly season with salt and pepper. Spray with avocado oil spray on all sides and transfer to the air fryer basket.

> **400°F   air fry   8 mins**

3 Flip tofu. In a mixing bowl, toss broccoli, mushrooms, and bell pepper in lemon juice and onion powder. Lightly season with salt and pepper. Spray with avocado oil spray, toss, and spray again.

4 If you have room, place vegetables beside tofu in the air fryer basket. Otherwise, place atop a metal rack over the tofu.

> **400°F   air fry   10–12 mins**

5 Cook just until broccoli is crisp tender and tofu begins to brown.

6 Meanwhile, prepare the spicy peanut sauce by whisking together all ingredients. Serve over the tofu, vegetables, and cooked brown rice.

Calories per serving: 435 · Fat: 18g · Net Carbs: 36.5g · Fiber: 11.5g · Sugars: 6g · Protein: 27g

Miso and Quinoa-Crusted Cod with Snap Peas

Active Prep Time: 10 mins · Cook Time: 12 mins · Serves: 2

In this recipe, cod is crusted with quinoa for a nutty, crispy texture. White miso (Japanese soy bean paste) adds a savory flavor in an easy but elegant meal. The air-roasted snap peas and additional cooked quinoa complete the dish for maximal flavor with minimal ingredients.

INGREDIENTS

8 ounces snap peas, ends trimmed

2 (6-ounce) cod fillets

Juice of $1/2$ lemon

2 teaspoons sesame oil

$3/4$ teaspoon ground ginger

$1/4$ teaspoon pepper

$1/4$ teaspoon garlic powder

$1/4$ teaspoon salt

2 tablespoons white miso paste

$1\,1/2$ cups cooked quinoa, divided

2 green onions, sliced

Mona's Tips

White miso paste is recommended, as red miso paste has a higher sodium content. It is sold both refrigerated (in the produce section) and shelf-stable in the Asian-foods section of the supermarket.

DIRECTIONS

1 Place snap peas in a mixing bowl and lay cod fillets out on a cutting board. Drizzle lemon juice and then sesame oil over the snap peas and cod.

2 Season snap peas and cod with an equal amount of the ground ginger and pepper. Season only the snap peas with the garlic powder and salt.

3 In a small mixing bowl, fold together miso paste and $1/4$ cup of the cooked quinoa before spreading over the top of each cod fillet.

4 Transfer the snap peas to the air fryer basket and top with the cod fillets.

375°F   air fry   10–12 mins

5 Cod is done when the quinoa begins to crisp, and the fish easily flakes with a fork. Serve topped with sliced green onions alongside the snap peas and remaining cooked quinoa.

Calories per serving: 440 · Fat: 8.5g · Net Carbs: 42.5g · Fiber: 6.5g · Sugars: 8g · Protein: 39.5g

Fajita Chicken Tacos with Pico de Gallo

Active Prep Time: 20 mins · Cook Time: 17 mins · Serves: 4

This is my daughter Rachel's favorite dinner and she just loves to make it with her fiance Adam! Each generous portion is 3 whole tacos. Rachel loves to change it up with shrimp too, and even adds some black beans. I just love her creativity!

INGREDIENTS

1 pound boneless, skinless chicken breasts

2 bell peppers, cored

1 tablespoon olive oil

Juice of $1/2$ lime

1 tablespoon Chili Spice Blend (see page 10)

$1/2$ teaspoon onion powder

$1/4$ teaspoon salt

1 Hass avocado, sliced

12 mini "street taco" corn tortillas, warmed

Pico de Gallo

4 Roma tomatoes, seeded and diced

$1/4$ cup diced red onion

1 small jalapeño pepper, diced

Juice of $1/2$ lime

2 tablespoons chopped fresh cilantro

1 teaspoon minced garlic

$1/4$ teaspoon salt

DIRECTIONS

1 Slice chicken and bell peppers into $3/4$-inch strips. Transfer to a mixing bowl and toss with olive oil, lime juice, spice blend, onion powder, and salt.

2 Transfer to the air fryer basket. Shake basket halfway through the cook time.

400°F   air fry   15–17 mins

3 Meanwhile, prepare the pico de gallo by folding together all ingredients.

4 Assemble the tacos by topping warmed street taco tortillas with an equal amount of the chicken, peppers, avocado, and pico de gallo. Each serving is 3 street tacos.

Mona's Tips

The best way to warm a corn tortilla is to simply place in a dry skillet over medium-high heat for 30 seconds on each side.

Calories per serving: 360 · Fat: 12g · Net Carbs: 24.5g · Fiber: 8.5g · Sugars: 7.5g · Protein: 30g

Eggplant Parmesan Stackers

Active Prep Time: 20 mins · Cook Time: 17 mins · Serves: 2

This is one of my hubby Doug's favorite meals, and I LOVE when he cooks it for me! Thanks to the magic of the air fryer, the eggplant comes out extra crispy using minimal oil. Instead of a large casserole, I create 2-slice stackers, which makes it easy to portion out! Plus, you are always ensured to get the crispy AND cheesy parts!

INGREDIENTS

2 large eggs

$1/4$ teaspoon each: salt and pepper

1 cup gluten-free breadcrumbs

2 teaspoons Mediterranean Spice Blend (see page 11)

1 medium eggplant, cut into 8 slices, about $1/2$-inch thick

Olive oil spray

1 cup no added sugar marinara sauce, warmed

2 tablespoons grated Parmesan cheese

$1/2$ cup shredded part-skim mozzarella cheese

4 cups zucchini noodles, steamed

Mona's Tips

Leaving the eggplant unpeeled will help the slices retain their shape after cooking. I like to partially stripe-peel mine to reduce bitterness.

DIRECTIONS

1 In a wide bowl, whisk together eggs, salt, and pepper. Mix breadcrumbs and spice blend in a separate wide bowl.

2 Dip the sliced eggplant in the egg mixture and then press into the breadcrumbs on both sides to fully coat.

3 Spray breaded eggplant on both sides with olive oil spray and transfer to the air fryer basket with the least amount of overlap.

400°F air fry 12 mins

4 Transfer 4 slices of cooked eggplant to a plate and top with a spoonful of marinara sauce, and then top the sauce with an equal amount of the Parmesan cheese. Place the other 4 slices of cooked eggplant over the first 4 to create short stacks of 2 (as pictured). Top each stack with another spoonful of sauce and an equal amount of mozzarella cheese. Return the 4 stacks to the air fryer.

400°F air fry 3–5 mins

5 Cook just until cheese is bubbly hot and eggplant is tender. Serve 2 eggplant stackers for each serving alongside an equal amount of steamed zucchini noodles.

Calories per serving: 475 · Fat: 17g · Net Carbs: 47g · Fiber: 13.5g · Sugars: 19g · Protein: 26.5g

Crispy Paella

Accessory: 7-inch baking dish · Active Prep Time: 15 mins · Cook Time: 20 mins · Serves: 2

The best part of a traditional paella is the crispy rice that forms at the bottom of the (stovetop) pan. This recipe flips that upside down by air frying the top of the rice to create a similar crispness with far less risk of burning. I then add my own nutritious spin by substituting cauliflower rice for half of the rice and using chicken sausage in place of andouille sausage. And don't worry... there's still shrimp in there!

INGREDIENTS

1 (8.8-ounce) pouch cooked yellow rice

12 ounces grated cauliflower rice

$3/4$ cup canned diced tomatoes, liquid drained

$1/4$ cup diced red onion

3 tablespoons chopped fresh parsley

Juice of $1/2$ lemon

2 teaspoons olive oil

2 teaspoons Roasting Spice Blend (see page 10)

1 bay leaf

$1/4$ teaspoon salt

$1/4$ teaspoon pepper

6 ounces frozen cooked shrimp

$2/3$ cup frozen peas

2 links smoked chicken sausage, sliced

Olive oil spray

DIRECTIONS

1 In a mixing bowl, fold together rice, cauliflower rice, tomatoes, onion, parsley, lemon juice, olive oil, spice blend, bay leaf, salt, and pepper.

2 Transfer the rice mixture to a 7-inch baking dish. Place baking dish in the air fryer basket.

325°F air fry 8 mins

3 Stir shrimp and peas into the rice and place sliced chicken sausage over top all to help with browning. Increase air fryer temperature.

350°F air fry 6 mins

4 Stir sausage into the rice, pat rice down, and spray the top with olive oil spray.

350°F air fry 5–6 mins

5 Paella is done when the rice on the top is slightly crisp.

Calories per serving: 485 · Fat: 11g · Net Carbs: 56.5g · Fiber: 10g · Sugars: 10.5g · Protein: 32.5g

Air-Roasted Beet and Bean Salad

Active Prep Time: 20 mins · Cook Time: 20 mins · Serves: 2–4

Air-roasted beets are the star of this uniquely satisfying salad topped with a rosemary vinaigrette. Clementine orange segments, cannellini beans, crumbled goat cheese, and pistachios all add unique textures and balanced flavors for a salad that is truly a full meal.

INGREDIENTS

Air-Roasted Beets

1 pound beets, trimmed and peeled

2 teaspoons olive oil

Salt and pepper

Salads

4 packed cups mixed greens

1 clementine orange,
   peeled and sectioned

1 cup canned cannellini beans,
   drained and rinsed

1/4 cup crumbled goat cheese

2 tablespoons pistachios

Rosemary Vinaigrette

1 tablespoon red wine vinegar

1 tablespoon extra-virgin olive oil

1 teaspoon Dijon mustard

1 teaspoon honey

1/4 teaspoon dried rosemary

DIRECTIONS

1 Cut small beets into quartered wedges and/or large beets into eighths. In a mixing bowl, toss with olive oil and lightly season with salt and pepper.

2 Transfer beets to the air fryer basket. Shake basket halfway through the cook time.

> **400°F   air fry   18–20 mins**

3 Beets are done when lightly browned and fork-tender.

4 Assemble 2 entrée salads or 4 appetizer salads by arranging an equal amount of the mixed greens across separate plates. Top with an equal amount of the roasted beets, orange sections, beans, goat cheese, and pistachios.

5 Prepare the rosemary vinaigrette by whisking together all ingredients. Drizzle over the salads before serving.

> **Mona's Tips**
>
> The roasted beets in this salad can be prepared as their own side dish for any meal. Up to 2 pounds (before peeling) of beets, regular or golden color, can be air fried in the same cook time.

Calories per serving: 405 · Fat: 18g · Net Carbs: 32.5g · Fiber: 14g · Sugars: 18g · Protein: 16g

Proteins

The Perfect Burger

Active Prep Time: 5 mins · Cook Time: 12 mins · Serves: 4

Whether you prefer lean ground beef, turkey, chicken, or keeping things plant-based, you can make a truly great burger in your air fryer! They come out perfectly juicy on the inside, with a delicious crispy crust.

INGREDIENTS

Avocado oil spray

1 pound lean ground beef, ground turkey, ground chicken, or raw plant-based burger

Salt and pepper

Gluten-free buns

Burger toppings

Flavor Mix-Ins

2 teaspoons Barbecue, Chili, or Mediterranean Spice Blend (see page 10–11)

2 teaspoons everything bagel seasoning

2 teaspoons taco seasoning

1 1/2 teaspoons Montreal steak seasoning

2 teaspoons ginger paste and 1 tablespoon gluten-free hoisin sauce

1 teaspoon garlic paste and 2 tablespoons chopped fresh herbs

1/4 cup crumbled or shredded cheese

DIRECTIONS

1 Spray air fryer basket with avocado oil spray. Use your hands to form ground meat into 4 burger patties, about 1/2-inch thick.

2 For more flavorful burgers (recommended for ground turkey or chicken), fold a flavor mix-in into the ground meat before forming burgers.

3 Spray burger patties with avocado oil spray on both sides and generously season with salt and pepper. Transfer to the air fryer basket. No need to flip the burgers as they cook. For frozen burger patties, increase cook time by 2–3 minutes.

> **400°F   air fry   8–12 mins**

4 Use a meat thermometer inserted into the center to check for doneness. Medium-rare beef or plant-based should cook 8–10 minutes and register 135°F. Medium-well should cook 9–11 minutes and register 150°F. Chicken or turkey burgers should cook 10–12 minutes and register 165°F.

5 To add cheese: Place over burgers as soon as they've finished cooking and leave in the warm air fryer, with heat off, for 1 minute.

6 Serve the patties as part of a bunless burger platter with salad greens and vegetables or atop your favorite bun with your choice of toppings.

Calories per lean beef burger patty: 170 · Fat: 8g · Net Carbs: 0g · Fiber: 0g · Sugars: 0g · Protein: 23g

Salmon Burgers

Active Prep Time: 10 mins · Cook Time: 12 mins · Serves: 4

Fresh salmon fillets are chopped and mixed with Dijon mustard, lemon, capers, dill, and parsley to make these amazing salmon burgers!

INGREDIENTS

1 pound skinless salmon
  fillets, chopped

Zest of $1/2$ lemon

2 tablespoons chopped
  fresh parsley

2 tablespoons chopped fresh dill

1 tablespoon capers

1 tablespoon Dijon mustard

$1/4$ teaspoon pepper

$1/2$ cup gluten-free panko
  breadcrumbs, plus
  additional to coat

Olive oil spray

Mona's Tips

These burgers are perfectly topped with my homemade tartar sauce (see page 125) or remoulade sauce (see page 68).

DIRECTIONS

1 Place all ingredients, except olive oil spray, in a food processor and pulse just until salmon is finely minced and everything is combined.

2 Pour additional panko breadcrumbs out on a plate. Form the salmon mixture into 4 burger patties and press into the breadcrumbs on both sides.

3 Spray the burgers with olive oil spray on both sides and transfer to the air fryer basket.

350°F   air fry   10–12 mins

4 Salmon burgers are done when a meat thermometer inserted into the center registers 140°F.

5 Serve the patties as part of a bunless burger platter with salad greens and vegetables or atop your favorite bun with your choice of toppings.

Calories per serving: 265 · Fat: 7.5g · Net Carbs: 19g · Fiber: 2g · Sugars: 0.5g · Protein: 26g

Almond Chicken with Marmalade Sauce

Active Prep Time: 10 mins · Cook Time: 17 mins · Serves: 2

Boneless, skinless chicken breasts are crusted with a hint of Dijon mustard and sliced almonds in this entrée that pack a satisfying crunch! I like to top it with a sweet and savory sauce made with orange marmalade.

INGREDIENTS

Olive oil spray

2 (6-ounce) boneless, skinless chicken breast fillets

Salt and pepper

1 egg yolk

2 teaspoons Dijon mustard

1/4 teaspoon dried rosemary

1/4 cup raw sliced almonds

Marmalade Sauce

1/4 cup chicken stock

2 tablespoons reduced-sugar orange marmalade

2 teaspoons Dijon mustard

1 teaspoon cornstarch

1 tablespoon cold water

Mona's Tips

The simple marmalade sauce is also great when made with apricot or peach preserves.

DIRECTIONS

1 Spray the air fryer basket with olive oil spray.

2 Season both sides of the chicken breasts with salt and pepper.

3 In a small mixing bowl, whisk together egg yolk, Dijon mustard, and rosemary. Brush over the tops of each chicken breast.

4 Press the sliced almonds into the egg yolk mixture to fully coat the top of each chicken breast. Transfer to the air fryer basket.

325°F   air fry   15–17 mins

5 Chicken is done when a meat thermometer inserted into the thickest part registers 165°F.

6 Meanwhile, prepare the marmalade sauce by whisking together chicken stock, marmalade, and Dijon mustard in a small saucepan on the stovetop over medium heat. Bring up to a simmer.

7 Whisk cornstarch into 1 tablespoon of cold water and then whisk into the simmering sauce. Stirring constantly, let simmer 3 minutes. Serve over the cooked chicken.

Calories per serving: 315 · Fat: 10g · Net Carbs: 10g · Fiber: 2g · Sugars: 7g · Protein: 43.5g

Sirloin Steak with Red Wine Reduction

Active Prep Time: 5 mins · Cook Time: 14 mins · Serves: 2

The air fryer is one of the simplest ways to perfectly prepare a flavorful steak. For even more flavor, try it with my recipe for a red wine reduction with onions.

INGREDIENTS

2 top sirloin steaks,
   about 1-inch thick

Olive oil spray

Salt, pepper, and garlic powder

Red Wine Reduction

2 teaspoons olive oil

$1/2$ cup sliced red onion

$1/2$ teaspoon dried rosemary

$1/2$ cup dry red wine

$1/4$ cup beef stock

$1/2$ tablespoon butter

Mona's Tips

This same cook time and method will work for up to 1 pound of any steaks that are 1-inch thick. I prefer top sirloin, as it is lean, tender, a good value, and easy to find in a thick cut.

DIRECTIONS

1 Pat steaks dry with paper towels. Spray both sides with olive oil spray and generously season with salt, pepper, and garlic powder.

2 Transfer to the air fryer basket. Flip steaks halfway through the cook time.

400°F air fry 9–14 mins

3 Use a meat thermometer inserted into the center to check for doneness. Medium-rare should cook 9–11 minutes and register 135°F. Medium should cook 11–13 minutes and register 145°F. Medium-well should cook 13–14 minutes and register 150°F. Reduce cook times by 2 minutes for $3/4$-inch-thick steaks.

4 Meanwhile, prepare the red wine reduction by heating olive oil in a small saucepan on the stovetop over medium heat. Add onions and rosemary and sauté 5 minutes, until onions are translucent.

5 Pour in red wine and beef stock and bring up to a simmer. Let simmer 10 minutes, or until liquid has reduced by half.

6 Remove from heat, stir in butter, and serve drizzled over the cooked steaks.

Calories per 4 ounces steak: 210 · Fat: 12g · Net Carbs: 0g · Fiber: 0g · Sugars: 0g · Protein: 23g

Calories in $1/2$ red wine reduction: 95 · Fat: 3g · Net Carbs: 5.5g · Fiber: 0.5g · Sugars: 2g · Protein: 1g

Blackened White Fish

Active Prep Time: 5 mins · Cook Time: 11 mins · Serves: 2

One of my favorite ways to season fish is to use my homemade and robust blackening blend made using spice rack staples. My particular blend of spices is full of flavor but only mildly spicy. For more heat, double the amount of ground cayenne pepper.

INGREDIENTS

Olive oil spray

2 (6-ounce) cod, or any white fish, fillets

Lemon wedges, optional

Blackening Blend

$1/2$ teaspoon paprika

$1/4$ teaspoon dried thyme

$1/4$ teaspoon garlic powder

$1/4$ teaspoon onion powder

$1/4$ teaspoon salt

$1/4$ teaspoon pepper

$1/8$ teaspoon ground cayenne pepper

Mona's Tips

This same cook time can be used to prepare white fish with any spices of your choosing.

DIRECTIONS

1 Spray air fryer basket and fish fillets with olive oil spray.

2 In a small mixing bowl, combine all blackening blend spices before generously seasoning the fish on both sides. Lightly spray the spices on top of the fish with additional olive oil spray.

3 Transfer to the air fryer basket.

375°F air fry 9–11 mins

4 Fish is done when the fish easily flakes with a fork. Serve with lemon wedges to squeeze over top.

Calories per serving: 150 · Fat: 2g · Net Carbs: 1g · Fiber: 0g · Sugars: 0g · Protein: 28.5g

Meatballs with Marinara Sauce

Active Prep Time: 20 mins · Cook Time: 20 mins · Serves: 4

These Italian meatballs are made with extra-lean ground beef but kept moist by a flavorful, yet simple, homemade marinara sauce (included in the nutritional information)!

INGREDIENTS

Olive oil spray

Marinara Sauce

1 tablespoon olive oil

$1/2$ yellow onion, diced

1 tablespoon minced garlic

1 (28-ounce) can crushed San Marzano tomatoes

1 teaspoon dried oregano

$1/2$ teaspoon salt

$1/2$ teaspoon pepper

$1/4$ cup chopped fresh basil

Meatballs

1 pound extra-lean (or plant-based) ground beef

1 large egg, beaten

$1/4$ cup gluten-free breadcrumbs

2 tablespoons chopped fresh parsley

2 teaspoons minced garlic

2 teaspoons Mediterranean Spice Blend (see page 11)

$1/2$ teaspoon salt

$1/2$ teaspoon pepper

DIRECTIONS

1 Spray the air fryer basket with olive oil spray.

2 Prepare the marinara sauce by placing olive oil in a pot on the stovetop over medium heat. Add onion and sauté 5 minutes, until translucent. Stir in garlic and sauté 1 additional minute.

3 Add crushed tomatoes, oregano, salt, and pepper and bring up to a simmer. Reduce heat to medium-low and, stirring occasionally, let simmer 20 minutes. Stir in fresh basil in the last 5 minutes of the cook time.

4 In a mixing bowl, use your hands to combine all meatball ingredients.

5 Form the meatball mixture into golf ball–sized balls and place in the air fryer in as close to a single layer as possible. It is okay to place a few in a second layer. Spray tops with olive oil spray.

6 Flip the meatballs halfway through the cook time.

375°F   air fry   12–14 mins

7 Meatballs are done when lightly browned and a meat thermometer registers 155°F.

8 Add meatballs to the simmering marinara sauce and let cook 1 minute before serving.

Calories per serving: 290 · Fat: 10g · Net Carbs: 15.5g · Fiber: 4g · Sugars: 7.5g · Protein: 30g

Apricot and Mustard Glazed Salmon

Active Prep Time: 5 mins · Cook Time: 12 mins · Serves: 2

This super-simple recipe uses only two pantry staples to make a sweet and savory glaze for perfectly air fried salmon! The secret to using so few ingredients is the whole-grain (deli) mustard that adds acid, spice, and salt to the sweet apricot preserves.

INGREDIENTS

Olive oil spray

2 (5-ounce) salmon fillets

$1/2$ teaspoon ground ginger

$1/2$ teaspoon cumin

3 tablespoons apricot preserves

$1\,^{1}/_{2}$ tablespoons mild whole-grain mustard

Mona's Tips

When cooking fish, always spray your air fryer basket with olive or avocado oil spray, as well as the fish, to prevent sticking.

DIRECTIONS

1 Spray air fryer basket and salmon fillets with olive oil spray. Season fillets with ground ginger and cumin. Transfer to the air fryer basket.

> **400°F   air fry   6 mins**

2 In a small mixing bowl, stir together apricot preserves and whole-grain mustard to make a glaze.

3 Spoon a thick layer of the glaze over the partially cooked salmon and continue cooking.

> **400°F   air fry   4–6 mins**

4 Salmon is done when glaze is bubbly hot and the fish easily flakes with a fork.

Calories per serving: 265 · Fat: 9g · Net Carbs: 11g · Fiber: 0g · Sugars: 9.5g · Protein: 30.5g

Italian Chicken Breasts from Fresh or Frozen

Active Prep Time: 5 mins · Cook Time: 18 mins · Serves: 2

Whether fresh or frozen, the air fryer can cook a perfect boneless, skinless chicken breast in under 20 minutes! I love to make them with a flavorful Italian rub (included in the nutritional information), but these same times and temperatures can be used with any seasoning or spice rub.

INGREDIENTS

2 (6-ounce) boneless, skinless chicken breast fillets, fresh or frozen

Olive oil spray, for frozen chicken

Italian Rub

1 tablespoon extra-virgin olive oil

2 teaspoons lemon zest

2 teaspoons Mediterranean Spice Blend (see page 11)

1 teaspoon red wine vinegar

$1/2$ teaspoon sugar

$1/2$ teaspoon garlic powder

$1/4$ teaspoon paprika

$1/4$ teaspoon salt

$1/4$ teaspoon pepper

Mona's Tips

This same recipe can be made with boneless, skinless chicken thighs by reducing the cook time by 2 minutes.

DIRECTIONS

1 Add all Italian rub ingredients to a small mixing bowl and combine.

Fresh Chicken

2 Spread the Italian rub over the entire surface of the chicken breasts.

3 Transfer to the air fryer basket. There is no need to flip during the cook time.

> 375°F air fry 12–15 mins

4 Chicken is done when a meat thermometer inserted into the thickest part registers 165°F.

Frozen Chicken

Spray air fryer basket with olive oil spray and place frozen chicken breasts inside. Cook for the first 5 minutes of the cook time below to partially thaw. Brush the chicken with the Italian rub and continue cooking until a meat thermometer inserted into the thickest part registers 165°F.

> 350°F air fry 15–18 mins

Calories with rub: 245 · Fat: 8g · Net Carbs: 1.5g · Fiber: 0g · Sugars: 1.5g · Protein: 39g

Seasoned or Breaded Pork Chops

Active Prep Time: 5 mins · Cook Time: 14 mins · Serves: 2

Breaded or simply well-seasoned, center cut pork chops are lean cuts of pork that are quick to prep and maybe even quicker to cook!

INGREDIENTS

Olive oil spray

2 (5-ounce) boneless
   pork loin chops

Seasoned

Salt and pepper, Italian
   Rub (see page 118), or
   1–2 teaspoons of your favorite
   spice blend/seasoning

Breaded

1 large egg

1 teaspoon Mediterranean
   Spice Blend (see page 11)

$1/4$ teaspoon salt

$1/4$ teaspoon pepper

1 cup gluten-free
   seasoned breadcrumbs

Mona's Tips

This same method can be used to cook 4 pork chops by increasing the cook time by 2 minutes.

DIRECTIONS

1 Spray air fryer basket with olive oil spray.

2 For seasoned pork chops, spray both sides with olive oil spray and generously season with salt and pepper or your favorite rub or spice blend.

3 For breaded pork chops, whisk together egg, spice blend, salt, and pepper in a wide bowl. Place breadcrumbs in a separate wide bowl. Dip the pork chops in the egg and then press into the breadcrumbs on both sides to coat. Generously spray with olive oil spray on both sides.

4 Transfer pork chops to the air fryer basket. Flip halfway through the cook time.

Seasoned

> 375°F   air fry   10–12 mins

Breaded

> 350°F   air fry   12–14 mins

5 Pork is done when a meat thermometer inserted into the thickest part registers 145°F.

Calories per seasoned chop: 210 · Fat: 9g · Net Carbs: 0.5g · Fiber: 0g · Sugars: 0g · Protein: 30.5g

Calories per breaded chop: 295 · Fat: 11g · Net Carbs: 13g · Fiber: 1g · Sugars: 1g · Protein: 34g

Tofu Two Ways

Active Prep Time: 15 mins · Cook Time: 17 mins · Serves: 4

Crispy air fried tofu makes for a fantastic protein to top Asian, Southwestern, or Mediterranean rice/grain bowls. For the most flavor, I like to either spice-rub the tofu before cooking or glaze it after.

INGREDIENTS

14–16 ounces extra-firm tofu

1 tablespoon cornstarch

Avocado oil spray

Spice-Rubbed Tofu

1 tablespoon any spice blend
   (see pages: 10–11)

1/2 teaspoon salt

Glazed Tofu

1 teaspoon ground ginger

1/2 teaspoon pepper

Ginger Soy Glaze

2 tablespoons water

2 tablespoons coconut aminos or
   reduced-sodium tamari soy sauce

1 tablespoon ginger paste

1 tablespoon rice wine vinegar

1 tablespoon honey

1 1/2 teaspoons cornstarch

1 tablespoon cold water

1 teaspoon sesame oil

DIRECTIONS

1 Press tofu between paper towels to remove excess water. Cut into 1-inch cubes and pat with additional paper towels.

2 Sprinkle tofu with cornstarch and desired spices on at least 2 sides. If you are making the glazed recipe, season with the ground ginger and black pepper.

3 Spray tofu with avocado oil spray on all sides and transfer to the air fryer basket. Flip halfway through the cook time.

400°F   air fry   15–17 mins

4 Tofu is done when it has slightly crisped and begun to brown. For spice-rubbed tofu, serve as is.

5 For glazed tofu, prepare the ginger soy glaze by whisking together 2 tablespoons of water, aminos, ginger paste, rice wine vinegar, and honey in a small saucepan on the stovetop over medium heat. Bring up to a simmer.

6 Whisk cornstarch into 1 tablespoon of cold water and then whisk into the simmering glaze. Stirring constantly, let simmer 1 minute. Remove from heat and stir in sesame oil. Toss the cooked tofu in the glaze before serving.

Calories per spice-rubbed serving: 145 · Fat: 7g · Net Carbs: 4g · Fiber: 0g · Sugars: 0g · Protein: 15g

Calories per glazed serving: 185 · Fat: 8g · Net Carbs: 11g · Fiber: 0g · Sugars: 5.5g · Protein: 15.5g

Air Fried Fish

Active Prep Time: 10 mins · Cook Time: 12 mins · Serves: 2

Cod, or any white fish, fillets are breaded and air fried to perfection in this family favorite! Serve alongside lemons, malt vinegar, or homemade tartar sauce (included in the nutritional information). Make this fish and chips by first air frying French fries (see page 130) and setting aside. Add cooked fries to the fish in the last minute of cooking to reheat.

INGREDIENTS

1 large egg

2 tablespoons gluten-free flour

1 teaspoon honey

$1/4$ teaspoon salt

1 cup gluten-free breadcrumbs

2 cod, or any white fish, fillets (about 6 ounces each)

Avocado oil spray

Homemade Tartar Sauce

2 tablespoons nonfat plain Greek yogurt

$1 1/2$ tablespoons olive oil or avocado oil mayonnaise

2 teaspoons dill relish

1 teaspoon Dijon mustard

1 teaspoon honey

$1/2$ teaspoon lemon juice

$1/4$ teaspoon dried dill

$1/4$ teaspoon onion powder

Pinch pepper

DIRECTIONS

1 In a wide bowl, whisk together egg, flour, honey, and salt. Place breadcrumbs in a separate wide bowl.

2 Dip the fish fillets in the egg mixture and then press into the breadcrumbs on both sides, to coat.

3 Spray breaded fish with avocado oil spray on both sides. Transfer to the air fryer basket. Flip halfway through the cook time.

> **350°F   air fry   10–12 mins**

4 Fish is done when breading is golden brown and interior is opaque throughout.

5 Meanwhile, prepare the homemade tartar sauce by stirring together all ingredients. Serve alongside the fried fish.

> **Mona's Tips**
>
> Most olive oil or avocado oil mayonnaises are lower in fat. Look for a brand with 5–7 grams of fat per serving.

Calories per serving: 355 · Fat: 9g · Net Carbs: 32g · Fiber: 2g · Sugars: 7.5g · Protein: 35.5g

"Rotisserie" Chicken

Active Prep Time: 10 mins · Cook Time: 1+ hour · Serves: 4–6

With this whole chicken recipe, you can get "rotisserie" results, right from your air fryer! The secret is starting the chicken breast-side down to ensure the meat cooks evenly without drying out.

INGREDIENTS

Olive oil spray

1 small whole chicken
   (about 3.5 pounds)

Juice of $1/2$ lemon

2 teaspoons paprika

1 teaspoon dried thyme

$3/4$ teaspoon onion powder

$1/2$ teaspoon oregano

$1/2$ teaspoon ground sage

$1/2$ teaspoon salt

$1/2$ teaspoon pepper

Mona's Tips

This recipe is only recommended for extra-large air fryers. Please be conscious of any maximum-fill line or maximum-height on your air fryer to ensure that the chicken is not taller than your machine allows.

DIRECTIONS

1 Spray the air fryer basket with olive oil spray.

2 Rinse chicken and remove any giblets. Pat dry with paper towels.

3 For the most even cooking, tuck the wings under the breast and tie the back legs together with baking twine.

4 Squeeze lemon juice over the chicken and spray with olive oil spray. Combine all remaining spice ingredients and rub over every surface of the bird.

5 Transfer to the air fryer basket breast-side down.

   350°F   air fry   35 mins

6 Using 2 heavy forks, carefully flip the chicken breast-side up to continue cooking.

   350°F   air fry   25–30 mins

7 Chicken is done when a meat thermometer inserted between the breast and the leg registers 165°F. Let rest 10 minutes before carving.

Calories per 6 ounces with skin: 320 · Fat: 16g · Net Carbs: 0g · Fiber: 0g · Sugars: 0g · Protein: 44g

Veggies

Classic French Fries

Active Prep Time: 15 mins · Cook Time: 20 mins · Serves: 2

French fries are the ultimate air fryer food! You get crispy results from fresh potatoes with around a third of the fat found in most frozen French fries before cooking (which are pre-fried before freezing).

INGREDIENTS

1 large russet potato

Olive oil spray

Salt, to taste

Mona's Tips

This method can be used to make larger quantities in multiple batches. Simply cut and soak multiple potatoes at the same time and remove enough from the water to air fry in close to a single layer. The rest of the potatoes can continue soaking until they are ready to be cooked.

DIRECTIONS

1 Scrub and dry potato. Cut lengthwise into ½-inch thick fries.

2 Place fries in a bowl of cold water and let soak for 1 hour, draining and replacing the cold water at least once.

3 Transfer to paper towels to pat dry and then transfer to the air fryer basket. Spray with olive oil spray on all sides. Shake basket halfway through the cook time.

375°F air fry 12 mins

4 Spray fries with additional olive oil spray on both sides. Increase temperature and continue cooking. Shake basket halfway through the cook time.

400°F air fry 6–8 mins

5 Fries are done when tender on the inside and crispy on the outside. Season with salt to taste while still hot.

Calories per serving: 150 · Fat: 4.5g · Net Carbs: 24g · Fiber: 2g · Sugars: 1g · Protein: 3g

Sweet Potato Fries

Active Prep Time: 15 mins · Cook Time: 16 mins · Serves: 2

The secret to making homemade sweet potato fries crispy is a light dusting of cornstarch before air frying. It absorbs some of the moisture as the fries cook and adds just enough starch to lightly brown.

INGREDIENTS

1 large sweet potato

Olive oil spray

2 teaspoons cornstarch

Salt, to taste

Mona's Tips

This method can be used to make larger quantities in multiple batches. Simply cut and soak multiple potatoes at the same time and remove enough from the water to air fry in close to a single layer. The rest of the potatoes can continue soaking until they are ready to be cooked.

DIRECTIONS

1 Scrub and dry sweet potato. Cut lengthwise into $1/2$-inch thick fries.

2 Place fries in a bowl of cold water and let soak for 1 hour, draining and replacing the cold water at least once.

3 Transfer to paper towels to pat dry and then transfer to the air fryer basket. Spray with olive oil spray on all sides. Sprinkle with cornstarch and spray with olive oil spray again. Shake basket halfway through the cook time.

375°F   air fry   8 mins

4 Spray fries with additional olive oil spray on both sides. Increase temperature and continue cooking. Shake basket halfway through the cook time.

400°F   air fry   6–8 mins

5 Fries are done when tender on the inside and crispy on the outside. Season with salt to taste while still hot.

Calories per serving: 150 · Fat: 4.5g
Net Carbs: 22g · Fiber: 4g
Sugars: 5.5g · Protein: 2g

Mediterranean Eggplant

Active Prep Time: 10 mins · Cook Time: 20 mins · Serves: 4

Eggplant, bell pepper, and red onion are seasoned with a splash of lemon, garlic, and my Mediterranean Spice Blend in this surprisingly low-calorie, colorful, and fiber-filled side dish.

INGREDIENTS

1 medium eggplant

1 red bell pepper, cored

$1/2$ red onion

1 tablespoon olive oil

Juice of $1/2$ lemon

2 teaspoons Mediterranean Spice Blend (see page 11)

$1/2$ teaspoon garlic powder

$1/4$ teaspoon salt

$1/4$ teaspoon pepper

Mona's Tips

The eggplant can be peeled or stripe-peeled before cutting into cubes, according to your preference. I like to stripe-peel mine to reduce bitterness.

DIRECTIONS

1 Cut and discard ends from eggplant before cutting into 1-inch cubes. Chop bell pepper and onion into 1-inch pieces.

2 In a large mixing bowl, toss the chopped vegetables in olive oil, lemon juice, spice blend, garlic powder, salt, and pepper.

3 Transfer to the air fryer basket. Shake basket halfway through the cook time.

400°F   air fry   18–20 mins

4 Eggplant is done when fork-tender and beginning to brown.

Calories per serving: 90 · Fat: 4g · Net Carbs: 7g · Fiber: 7g · Sugars: 6g · Protein: 2.5g

Curry Cauliflower

Active Prep Time: 10 mins · Cook Time: 12 mins · Serves: 4

Roasted cauliflower has such an amazing flavor that is nutty and slightly sweet. Seasoning with savory curry powder and spicy crushed red pepper flakes adds even more depth of flavor for a side dish that goes great with any Indian, Asian, or grilled meal. For an even simpler cauliflower recipe that goes with American or Mediterranean dishes, the curry powder can be omitted.

INGREDIENTS

1 tablespoon olive oil

1 tablespoon curry powder, divided

1 teaspoon lemon juice

$1/2$ teaspoon onion powder

$1/4$ teaspoon salt

$1/4$ teaspoon pepper

$1/8$ teaspoon crushed
red pepper flakes

1 head cauliflower, cut into florets

Mona's Tips

You can also roast frozen cauliflower in the air fryer in the same amount of time, but the final result won't be as crisp or browned. The oil and seasoning will coat the frozen cauliflower better if tossed $1/3$ of the way into the cook time, once the cauliflower is thawed on the outside.

DIRECTIONS

1 In a small mixing bowl, whisk together olive oil, $1/2$ tablespoon of the curry powder, lemon juice, onion powder, salt, pepper, and crushed red pepper flakes.

2 In a large mixing bowl, drizzle the seasoned olive oil over the cauliflower florets and toss to coat all. Sprinkle with the remaining $1/2$ tablespoon of curry powder and toss again.

3 Transfer to the air fryer basket.

400°F   air fry   10–12 mins

4 Cauliflower is done when crisp-tender and beginning to brown.

Calories per serving: 70 · Fat: 3.5g · Net Carbs: 4.5g · Fiber: 4g · Sugars: 3.5g · Protein: 3g

Crispy Brussels Sprouts

Active Prep Time: 10 mins · Cook Time: 17 mins · Serves: 4

These Brussels sprouts are my absolute FAVORITE thing to make in the air fryer and it's the only way that I now prepare them. The crispy texture far surpasses what you get in the oven, and in less time! Even if you think you don't like Brussels sprouts, I believe that this preparation will change your mind.

INGREDIENTS

1 pound Brussels sprouts, halved

1 tablespoon olive oil

2 teaspoons balsamic vinegar

$1/4$ teaspoon garlic powder

$1/4$ teaspoon salt

$1/4$ teaspoon pepper

DIRECTIONS

1 In a mixing bowl, toss halved Brussels sprouts with olive oil, balsamic vinegar, garlic powder, salt, and pepper.

2 Transfer to the air fryer basket. Shake basket halfway through the cook time.

> **400°F   air fry   15–17 mins**

3 Brussels sprouts are done when fork-tender and golden-brown.

Calories per serving: 80 · Fat: 3.5g · Net Carbs: 6g · Fiber: 4.5g · Sugars: 3g · Protein: 4g

Air-Roasted Asparagus

Active Prep Time: 5 mins · Cook Time: 8 mins · Serves: 4

Roasted asparagus is a simple side dish that you can air fry in just a few minutes before or after air frying the main course. They cook so quick that they can be made in the time it takes most cuts of meat to properly rest.

INGREDIENTS

1 pound asparagus

1 tablespoon olive oil

$1/2$ teaspoon garlic powder

$1/4$ teaspoon salt

$1/4$ teaspoon pepper

Lemon wedges, optional

Calories per serving: 55 · Fat: 3.5g
Net Carbs: 2g · Fiber: 2.5g
Sugars: 2g · Protein: 2.5g

DIRECTIONS

1 Trim and discard at least 1 inch from the stalk end of the asparagus.

2 Drizzle asparagus with olive oil and flip to coat on all sides. Season with garlic powder, salt, and pepper.

> **375°F air fry 5–8 mins**

3 Asparagus is done when stalks are crisp-tender. Serve with a squeeze of fresh lemon, if desired.

Veggie Fried Rice

Accessory: 7-inch baking dish · Active Prep Time: 10 mins · Cook Time: 20 mins · Serves: 4

This veggie-packed fried rice is air fried all in one baking dish! I make this recipe easy by buying a pouch of precooked rice, fresh pre-grated cauliflower rice, sliced mushrooms, and pre-shredded broccoli slaw.

INGREDIENTS

2 cups cooked brown rice

12 ounces grated cauliflower rice

1 1/2 tablespoons coconut aminos or reduced-sodium tamari soy sauce

1 tablespoon gluten-free hoisin sauce

2 teaspoons ginger paste

1 teaspoon minced garlic

1 tablespoon sesame oil

1/4 teaspoon onion powder

1 cup shredded broccoli slaw

4 ounces baby bella mushrooms, halved

Avocado oil spray

2 green onions, sliced

Mona's Tips

Hoisin sauce contains a small amount of wheat, but gluten-free hoisin is available. In a pinch, gluten-free teriyaki marinade can be substituted.

DIRECTIONS

1 In a mixing bowl, toss together brown rice, cauliflower rice, coconut aminos, hoisin sauce, ginger paste, garlic, sesame oil, and onion powder.

2 Transfer the rice mixture to a 7-inch baking dish. Top with the broccoli slaw and mushrooms and spray vegetables with avocado oil spray. Do not stir.

3 Place baking dish in the air fryer basket.

375°F   air fry   10 mins

4 Stir the vegetables into the rice and continue cooking. Stir halfway through the cook time.

375°F   air fry   8–10 mins

5 Fried rice is done when cauliflower is tender and the rice on the top begins to lightly brown. Serve topped with sliced green onions.

Calories per serving: 270 · Fat: 6.5g · Net Carbs: 42g · Fiber: 5g · Sugars: 6.5g · Protein: 7g

Crispy Veggie Noodle Nests

Active Prep Time: 10 mins · Cook Time: 10 mins · Serves: 2

Spiralized zucchini or butternut squash cook up crispy on the outside and tender on the inside in this unique side dish, snack, or crunchy salad topper!

INGREDIENTS

Zucchini Noodles

10 ounces spiralized zucchini (about 2 cups)

2 teaspoons olive oil

1 teaspoon Mediterranean Spice Blend (see page 11)

$1/4$ teaspoon garlic powder

$1/4$ teaspoon salt

$1/4$ teaspoon pepper

2 tablespoons shredded Parmesan cheese

Butternut Squash Noodles

10 ounces spiralized butternut squash (about 2 cups)

2 teaspoons olive oil

$1/2$ teaspoon ground cinnamon

$1/2$ teaspoon ground cumin

$1/4$ teaspoon salt

$1/4$ teaspoon pepper

DIRECTIONS

1 In a mixing bowl, toss zucchini or butternut squash in olive oil and spices.

2 Split into 6 portions and transfer to the air fryer basket in small round "nests." For smaller air fryers, you may need to cook in 2 batches of 3.

3 For zucchini noodles, top each nest with a sprinkling of shredded Parmesan cheese.

400°F air fry 8–10 mins

4 Noodles are done when crispy and well browned around the edges. Let rest 3 minutes before removing with a spatula.

Mona's Tips

I've made these in my bucket-style air fryer without issue, but they are even easier when made with a sheet pan air fryer.

Calories per zucchini serving: 85 · Fat: 6g · Net Carbs: 3.5g · Fiber: 1.5g · Sugars: 2g · Protein: 3.5g

Calories per butternut serving: 90 · Fat: 4.5g · Net Carbs: 10g · Fiber: 2.5g · Sugars: 3g · Protein: 2.5g

Balsamic Green Beans

Active Prep Time: 10 mins · Cook Time: 14 mins · Serves: 4

These air-roasted green beans get beautifully caramelized thanks to the sweet and tangy balsamic glaze. It's a simple and satisfying side dish that is on my dinner plate every week!

INGREDIENTS

1 pound green beans

2 teaspoons olive oil

2 teaspoons balsamic glaze

$1/4$ teaspoon dried rosemary

$1/4$ teaspoon garlic powder

$1/4$ teaspoon salt

$1/4$ teaspoon pepper

Mona's Tips

For plain roasted green beans, you can omit the balsamic glaze and rosemary; however, the glaze really helps the beans brown as they cook.

DIRECTIONS

1 Snap and discard ends from green beans.

2 In a mixing bowl, toss green beans with olive oil, balsamic glaze, rosemary, garlic powder, salt, and pepper.

3 Transfer to the air fryer basket. Do not flip green beans as they cook.

400°F air fry 12–14 mins

4 Green beans are done when tender and well browned on the top.

Calories per serving: 65 · Fat: 2.5g · Net Carbs: 6.5g · Fiber: 3.5g · Sugars: 3g · Protein: 2g

Maple Glazed Carrots

Active Prep Time: 5 mins · Cook Time: 18 mins · Serves: 4

While whole, peeled, carrots can be cut into $^3/_4$-inch-thick pieces for this recipe, I like to keep the prep-work simple by making these Maple Glazed Carrots with baby carrots. A bit of nutmeg adds a hint of earthy-ness that perfectly balances with the sweet maple syrup.

INGREDIENTS

1 pound baby carrots

1 teaspoon olive oil

1 tablespoon pure maple syrup, divided

$^1/_4$ teaspoon ground nutmeg

$^1/_4$ teaspoon salt

Mona's Tips

Ground cinnamon or ground cloves can be used in place of the nutmeg, depending on your tastes. For me, I like to use nutmeg, as it does not overpower the flavor of the maple syrup.

DIRECTIONS

1 In a mixing bowl, toss carrots in olive oil, $^1/_2$ of the maple syrup, nutmeg, and salt.

2 Transfer to the air fryer basket. Shake basket halfway through the cook time.

400°F air fry 16–18 mins

3 Carrots are done when fork-tender and beginning to brown.

4 Toss in the remaining $^1/_2$ tablespoon of maple syrup before serving.

Calories per serving: 70 · Fat: 1.5g · Net Carbs: 11g · Fiber: 3g · Sugars: 8g · Protein: 1g

Baked Potatoes

Active Prep Time: 5 mins · Cook Time: 50 mins · Serves: 1–4

The air fryer is the perfect way to make baked potatoes, as it takes less time and energy than using your traditional oven. The best part is that it makes the skin extra-extra-crispy, especially if you lightly oil them with olive oil before cooking.

INGREDIENTS

1–4 russet potatoes

Olive oil spray, optional

Topping Ideas

Butter

Greek yogurt or light sour cream

Chives or green onions

Turkey bacon

Shredded cheese

Salsa or guacamole

Chili

Smoked salmon

Reduced-fat cream cheese

Everything bagel seasoning

Pesto and Parmesan cheese

Tzatziki sauce

Calories per serving: 220 · Fat: 0g
Net Carbs: 48g · Fiber: 4g
Sugars: 2g · Protein: 6g

DIRECTIONS

1 Scrub and dry potatoes. Poke in several places with a fork.

2 For a crispy skin (optional), lightly spray on all sides with olive oil spray.

3 Transfer to the air fryer basket. Turn halfway through the cook time. For only 1 potato, reduce cook time by 5 minutes.

> **400°F air fry 45–50 mins**

4 Potatoes are done when fork-tender. Serve with your favorite toppings!

Baked Sweet Potatoes

Active Prep Time: 5 mins · Cook Time: 45 mins · Serves: 1–4

This is not just a nutritious side dish. I'll often make a baked sweet potato the star of a nutritious and satisfying lunch. I especially like to top them with mashed avocado for extra omega-3s and black beans for extra fiber and protein.

INGREDIENTS

1–4 medium sweet potatoes

Olive oil spray, optional

Topping Ideas

Butter

Greek yogurt

Pecans or walnuts

Pepitas or sunflower seeds

Ground cinnamon

Nutmeg

Curry powder

Maple syrup or honey

Black beans and salsa

Avocado

Almond butter

Turkey bacon

Ground turkey with cumin

Gorgonzola or goat cheese

Calories per serving: 170 · Fat: 0g
Net Carbs: 33g · Fiber: 6g
Sugars: 8g · Protein: 3g

DIRECTIONS

1 Scrub and dry potatoes. Poke in several places with a fork.

2 For a crispy skin (optional), lightly spray on all sides with olive oil spray.

3 Transfer to the air fryer basket. Turn halfway through the cook time. For only 1 potato, reduce cook time by 5 minutes.

> **400°F   air fry   40–45 mins**

4 Potatoes are done when fork-tender. Serve with your favorite toppings!

147

Baby Potatoes Two Ways

Active Prep Time: 5 mins · Cook Time: 25 mins · Serves: 4

Crispy air fried baby potatoes are one of my favorite side dishes! You can simply toss them in the air fryer with nearly no prep as you make the rest of your meal on the stove, oven, or grill. They're so quick and easy to make that I'll even start with roasted baby potatoes to make super flavorful smashed potatoes! Any color of baby potato can be used when roasting, but gold or redskin potatoes are recommended when smashing.

INGREDIENTS

Roasted

24 ounces baby potatoes

1 tablespoon olive oil

$^1/_4$ teaspoon salt

Roasted and Smashed

1 batch roasted baby potatoes (see above)

2 tablespoons nonfat plain Greek yogurt

2 tablespoons milk or plant-based milk

1 tablespoon butter

1 tablespoon grated Parmesan cheese

$^1/_4$ teaspoon garlic powder

$^1/_4$ teaspoon salt

$^1/_4$ teaspoon pepper

1 tablespoon chopped chives

DIRECTIONS

1 In a mixing bowl, toss potatoes in olive oil and salt.

2 Transfer to the air fryer basket. Shake basket halfway through the cook time.

> **400°F   air fry   22–25 mins**

3 Potatoes are done when crispy and fork-tender.

4 For smashed potatoes: Ensure potatoes are very tender before transferring to a mixing bowl while still hot.

5 Add yogurt, milk, butter, Parmesan cheese, garlic powder, salt, and pepper to the potatoes and mash with a potato masher, just until smooth and combined. If the potatoes are too thick, add additional milk until your desired consistency is reached.

6 Serve topped with chopped chives.

Calories per roasted serving: 135 · Fat: 3.5g
Net Carbs: 15g · Fiber: 3.5g · Sugars: 1g · Protein: 3.5g

Calories per smashed serving: 175 · Fat: 7g · Net Carbs: 16g · Fiber: 3.5g · Sugars: 1.5g · Protein: 5g

Root Veggie Fries with Smoked Ketchup

Active Prep Time: 15 mins · Cook Time: 20 mins · Serves: 4

Root veggie fries, with their natural sweetness, have quickly become my favorite choice in fries! Turnip, parsnip, and carrot sticks are air-roasted with a bit of cornstarch for extra crispiness. I like to dip them into smoked ketchup (included in the nutritional information), but you can also serve them with any dipping sauce of your choosing.

INGREDIENTS

$1/2$ pound turnips, peeled

$1/2$ pound parsnips, peeled

$1/2$ pound carrots, peeled

1 tablespoon olive oil

$1 1/2$ teaspoons cornstarch

$1/4$ teaspoon salt

$1/4$ teaspoon pepper

Smoked Ketchup

3 tablespoons tomato paste

2 tablespoons water

1 tablespoon white vinegar

1 tablespoon honey

2 teaspoons smoked paprika

$1/4$ teaspoon onion powder

$1/4$ teaspoon salt

DIRECTIONS

1 Cut root vegetables into $1/2$-inch thick sticks.

2 Toss vegetables in olive oil to fully coat before sprinkling with cornstarch, salt, and pepper.

3 Transfer to the air fryer basket. Shake basket halfway through the cook time.

400°F air fry 18–20 mins

4 Meanwhile, create the smoked ketchup by stirring together all ingredients. Serve alongside the cooked fries.

Mona's Tips

This method can be used to make fries from $1 1/2$ pounds of any of these three root vegetables on their own as well.

Calories per serving: 140 · Fat: 4g · Net Carbs: 20g · Fiber: 6g · Sugars: 12g · Protein: 2g

Air-Roasted Tomatoes

Active Prep Time: 5 mins · Cook Time: 15 mins · Serves: 4

Roasted tomatoes make a great lunchtime side dish, addition to caprese or tossed salads, or a unique and nutritious garnish for your next dinner! Compari tomatoes are the perfect size for roasting but Roma tomatoes that are halved lengthwise will also work.

INGREDIENTS

1 pound Compari or Roma tomatoes, halved

Olive oil spray

1/2 teaspoon Mediterranean Spice Blend (see page 11)

1/4 teaspoon garlic powder

1/4 teaspoon salt

1/4 teaspoon pepper

DIRECTIONS

1 Lightly spray halved tomatoes with olive oil spray before seasoning with all remaining ingredients.

2 Place tomatoes in the air fryer basket in a single layer.

> **400°F   air fry   13–15 mins**

Calories per serving: 40 · Fat: 2g · Net Carbs: 3g · Fiber: 1.5g · Sugars: 3g · Protein: 1g

Air-Roasted Radishes

Active Prep Time: 5 mins · Cook Time: 17 mins · Serves: 4

Move over potatoes! Looking for a lighter, lower-carb veggie with amazing texture and flavor? These radishes lightly caramelize on the outside and soften on the inside in a way that is surprisingly similar to baby potatoes with far, far less calories!

INGREDIENTS

1 pound radishes, trimmed and halved

2 teaspoons olive oil

$^1/_4$ teaspoon garlic powder

$^1/_4$ teaspoon salt

$^1/_4$ teaspoon pepper

1 tablespoon grated Parmesan cheese, optional

1 tablespoon chopped fresh parsley, optional

Calories per serving: 65 · Fat: 4g
Net Carbs: 2g · Fiber: 2g
Sugars: 2g · Protein: 2.5g

DIRECTIONS

1 In a mixing bowl, toss halved radishes in olive oil, garlic powder, salt, and pepper.

2 Place radishes in the air fryer basket in a single layer.

> **400°F   air fry   15–17 mins**

3 If desired, toss the roasted radishes in Parmesan cheese and parsley before serving.

153

Golden Corn on the Cob

Active Prep Time: 2 mins · Cook Time: 16 mins · Serves: 2–4

Whether you start with fresh or frozen corn on the cob, the air fryer can beautifully roast it for far more flavor than boiling or steaming! These are closer to grilled corn, without having to worry about the kernels burning before they're fully cooked.

INGREDIENTS

2–4 ears corn, fresh or frozen (may also use half-size or "nibbler" frozen corn)

Olive oil spray

Mona's Tips

Cooking 2 ears of corn will be on the shorter end of the cook time (around 13 minutes for fresh corn) and cooking 4 ears of corn will take a few minutes longer.

DIRECTIONS

1 If using fresh corn, shuck well before air frying.

2 Spray corn on all sides with olive oil spray.

3 Transfer to the air fryer basket. Turn halfway through the cook time. Cook until kernels are fork-tender.

Fresh Corn

375°F   air fry   13–15 mins

Frozen Corn

400°F   air fry   14–16 mins

Calories per serving: 85 · Fat: 1.5g · Net Carbs: 15g · Fiber: 2.5g · Sugars: 3g · Protein: 3g

Onion Rings with Sweet Chili Sauce

Active Prep Time: 15 mins · Cook Time: 14 mins · Serves: 4

These onion rings are made with both a batter to coat the onion and then breadcrumbs to keep the batter from dripping off in the air fryer basket. I like to dip them in a sweet chili sauce (included in the nutritional information), but they are also great all on their own!

INGREDIENTS

1 yellow onion, peeled

1 large egg

1 large egg white

2 tablespoons nonfat plain Greek yogurt

3 tablespoons gluten-free all-purpose flour

2 teaspoons light brown sugar

$1/2$ teaspoon salt

$1\,1/2$ cups gluten-free breadcrumbs

Olive oil spray

Sweet Chili Sauce

2 tablespoons tomato paste

$1\,1/2$ tablespoons water

1 tablespoon sriracha

2 teaspoons cider vinegar

2 teaspoons light brown sugar

1 teaspoon minced garlic

$1/4$ teaspoon crushed red pepper flakes

$1/4$ teaspoon salt

DIRECTIONS

1 Slice and separate onion into $1/2$-inch rings.

2 In a wide bowl, whisk together egg, egg white, yogurt, flour, sugar, and salt.

3 Place breadcrumbs in a separate wide bowl.

4 Flip the onion rings in the egg mixture to fully coat before pressing into the breadcrumbs on both sides.

5 Spray the breaded onion rings with olive oil spray on both sides. Place in the air fryer basket in as close to a single layer as possible. It is okay to overlap a few. For smaller air fryers you will have to cook in 2 batches. Use tongs to flip halfway through the cook time.

350°F air fry 12–14 mins

6 Meanwhile, create the sweet chili sauce by stirring together all ingredients. Serve alongside the cooked onion rings.

Calories per serving: 160 · Fat: 2.5g · Net Carbs: 28g · Fiber: 2g · Sugars: 8.5g · Protein: 6g

Desserts

Chocolate Chip Oatmeal Cookies

Active Prep Time: 10 mins · Cook Time: 8 mins · Serves: 8

One of my favorite uses of the air fryer is to make a small batch of fresh cookies for dessert time, any time. Each batch takes only 8 minutes to air-bake to crispy on the outside, soft on the inside, perfection! They're so fast, easy to make, and healthy-delicious!

INGREDIENTS

2 tablespoons coconut oil, melted

1 large egg white

$1/4$ cup light brown sugar

$1/2$ teaspoon vanilla extract

$1/4$ teaspoon ground cinnamon

$1/4$ teaspoon baking soda

Pinch salt

$1/3$ cup all-purpose gluten-free flour

$1/3$ cup rolled oats

2 tablespoons dark
  chocolate chips

Mona's Tips

Poking holes in the parchment paper allows some air to flow and cook the bottom of the cookies without the dough dripping through. If using a sheet pan air fryer, you can skip this step and simply cook on a solid sheet pan (which will retain heat to cook the bottom) rather than a basket.

DIRECTIONS

1 In a mixing bowl, whisk together melted coconut oil, egg white, brown sugar, vanilla extract, cinnamon, baking soda, and salt.

2 Fold flour and oats into the coconut oil mixture until a smooth dough is formed. Fold in chocolate chips. Refrigerate for 5 minutes.

3 Line the bottom of the air fryer with parchment paper and, using a toothpick, poke at least 12 holes in the paper to allow a small amount of air to flow through the paper.

4 For bucket-style air fryers, cook in 2 batches of 4 cookies. Large, sheet pan–style air fryers can be made in 1 batch of 8 cookies. Scoop 8 equal amounts of the chilled dough into the lined air fryer, as far apart as possible. Using a small piece of parchment paper, press down on the dough to flatten until around $3/4$-inch thick.

300°F   air fry   7–8 mins

5 Cookies are done when evenly golden brown. Leave inside air fryer, with the device off, for 3 minutes to cool before transferring basket to a rack to cool at least 5 additional minutes before serving.

Calories per cookie: 75 · Fat: 4g · Net Carbs: 9g · Fiber: 0.5g · Sugars: 5.5g · Protein: 1.5g

Ginger Caramelized Peaches with Pistachios

Active Prep Time: 5 mins · Cook Time: 7 mins · Serves: 2

This is my secret to getting the amazing flavor of a peach cobbler, without the extra fat and calories. Simply air fry the peaches with a light sweet and spiced coating of cinnamon, ginger, and a touch of brown sugar. The pistachio and whipped cream topping adds crunch and richness!

INGREDIENTS

2 peaches

3/4 teaspoon ground cinnamon

1/2 teaspoon ground ginger

1 tablespoon dark brown sugar

2 tablespoons chopped pistachios

Almond or coconut whipped cream, optional

Mona's Tips

Nectarines or peaches can be used interchangeably in this recipe. For firmer fruit (and less cleanup) after cooking, line the air fryer basket with parchment paper to place the peaches on top. This will slow the air flow and caramelize the tops of the peaches without fully baking the bottoms.

DIRECTIONS

1 Slice peaches in half around the pit, twisting to separate the halves. Use a sharp spoon to remove the pits.

2 Sprinkle each peach half with an equal amount of the cinnamon and ginger before topping with a light layer of brown sugar. Transfer halves, cut-side-up, to the air fryer basket.

> **400°F   air fry   5–7 mins**

3 Serve each peach half topped with chopped pistachios and a dollop of whipped cream, if desired.

Calories per serving: 100 · Fat: 3.5g · Net Carbs: 16g · Fiber: 3g · Sugars: 14.5g · Protein: 2.5g

Graham Cracker Apple Fries

Active Prep Time: 15 mins · Cook Time: 8 mins · Serves: 4

Gluten-free graham crackers can easily be found in the grocery store and then food-processed into crumbs to create a crunchy coating for apples in this simple dessert. This is a perfect family treat, especially when served with a drizzle of chocolate over top!

INGREDIENTS

2 medium apples

1 large egg white

1 tablespoon light brown sugar

$1/2$ teaspoon ground cinnamon

4 sheets gluten-free
  graham crackers

Avocado oil spray

Chocolate Drizzle

2 tablespoons dark chocolate

1 tablespoon unsweetened
  almond milk

Mona's Tips

For the best browning, lightly spray the apples with additional avocado oil after flipping halfway through the cook time.

DIRECTIONS

1 Peel, core, and slice apples into wedges around $1/2$-inch thick.

2 In a wide bowl, whisk together egg white, brown sugar, and cinnamon.

3 With a food processor, grind gluten-free graham crackers into a fine crumb before placing into a separate bowl.

4 Dip the apple wedges in the egg mixture before coating with graham cracker mixture on both sides. Continue until all coated and then spray with avocado oil spray on both sides. Place in the air fryer basket and cook, flipping halfway through.

400°F   air fry   7–8 mins

5 Create a chocolate drizzle by microwaving dark chocolate and almond milk in 10-second intervals, just until smooth and combined. Serve lightly drizzled over the graham cracker apples.

Calories per serving: 115 · Fat: 3g · Net Carbs: 20g · Fiber: 2.5g · Sugars: 16g · Protein: 2g

Mixed Berry Crumble

Accessory: 7-inch baking dish · Active Prep Time: 10 mins · Cook Time: 15 mins · Serves: 6

It's amazing how you can make this delicious crumble from frozen berries with only 15 minutes of cook time! The light buttery oat topping takes this dessert to the next level.

INGREDIENTS

Avocado oil spray

16 ounces frozen mixed berries

2 tablespoons light brown sugar

2 teaspoons cornstarch

1 tablespoon butter, melted

1 large egg white

1 1/2 tablespoons sugar

1/2 teaspoon ground cinnamon

Pinch salt

1/2 cup rolled oats

2 tablespoons gluten-free all-purpose flour

Vanilla Greek yogurt, to top, optional

Mona's Tips

This can also be made with 3 cups of fresh berries by increasing the temperature to 375°F and reducing the cook times to 3 minutes for the berries and then 6–8 minutes once topped with the crumble.

DIRECTIONS

1 Lightly spray a 7-inch baking dish with avocado oil spray.

2 Add frozen berries, brown sugar, and cornstarch to the baking dish and fold to evenly coat the berries. Place dish in the air fryer basket.

350°F air fry 5 mins

3 As the berries cook, make the crumble topping. In a mixing bowl, whisk together melted butter, egg white, sugar, cinnamon, and salt.

4 Fold in rolled oats and flour, until all is combined into a thick batter.

5 Stir the partially cooked berries in the baking dish and then top with spoonfuls of the crumble topping. Return dish to the air fryer basket.

350°F air fry 8–10 mins

6 Crumble is done when berries are bubbly hot and topping is crisp and lightly browned. Let rest 5 minutes before serving and top with dollops of vanilla yogurt, if desired.

Calories per serving: 120 · Fat: 2.5g · Net Carbs: 19g · Fiber: 4g · Sugars: 12.5g · Protein: 2g

Cinnamon Glazed Nuts

Active Prep Time: 5 mins · Cook Time: 10 mins · Serves: 6

I love the warm candied almonds at the local street fair festivals! The secret to making them at home using less sugar is an egg white coating, which adds crispiness without multiple coats of sugar. They're so good, I started making them with pecans and walnuts with equally satisfying results!

INGREDIENTS

2 $1/2$ tablespoons light brown sugar

1 tablespoon egg whites

$3/4$ teaspoon ground cinnamon

$1/4$ teaspoon vanilla extract

Pinch salt

1 cup raw almonds,
   or 1 $1/4$ cups raw walnuts,
   or 1 $1/4$ cups raw pecans

Mona's Tips

This is a great "last minute" dessert that can be made with baking walnuts, pecans, or almonds from the pantry and only a few other pantry staples!

DIRECTIONS

1 In a mixing bowl, whisk together brown sugar, egg whites, cinnamon, vanilla extract, and salt.

2 Fold almonds into the sugar mixture. Let rest 1 minute before folding again to ensure the almonds are fully coated. Transfer to the air fryer basket.

3 Lightly shake the basket every 3 minutes as the almonds cook.

325°F   air fry   8–10 mins

4 Almonds are done when they smell toasted and the sugar and egg white coating looks crisp. For the best texture, transfer to a bowl and let cool 10 minutes, as the coating gets crunchier as it cools. Store in an airtight container for up to 5 days.

Calories per serving: 130 · Fat: 9.5g · Net Carbs: 6g · Fiber: 3g · Sugars: 5.5g · Protein: 4.5g

Cheesecake Bites

Accessory: 7-cup silicone egg bite mold · Active Prep Time: 15 mins · Cook Time: 20 mins · Serves: 7

These bite-sized cheesecakes pack all the flavor of the full cake in an easy-to-portion dessert that is every bit as satisfying. Without a crust, these are naturally gluten-free but can be garnished with a piece of graham cracker (available gluten-free), if desired.

INGREDIENTS

Avocado oil spray

8 ounces reduced-fat cream cheese, softened

1 large egg

3 tablespoons sugar

1 tablespoon unsweetened almond milk

1/2 teaspoon lemon juice

1/2 teaspoon vanilla extract

Gluten-free graham crackers, berries, almond or coconut whipped cream, optional

Mona's Tips

Covering the silicone mold with aluminum foil is a must for this recipe, as cheesecakes are best cooked with even but gentle heat. The airflow in an air fryer is perfect for even, all-around heat, but aluminum foil will protect the top of the cakes from the most direct heat that comes from the heating element at the top.

DIRECTIONS

1 Lightly spray a 7-cup silicone egg bite mold with avocado oil spray.

2 For the best results, ensure cream cheese and egg have come to room temperature.

3 Using an electric mixer, beat all ingredients 2 minutes, until smooth.

4 Transfer the batter evenly between the 7 cups of the mold. Cover the silicone mold tightly with aluminum foil and place in the air fryer basket.

275°F air fry 18–20 mins

5 Cheesecakes are done when the edges are fully set and springy to the touch. The centers will be less firm and slightly sticky to the touch.

6 Remove from air fryer and let cool on a wire rack for 1 hour before refrigerating at least 4 hours. Serve with fresh berries, almond or coconut whipped cream, and/or gluten-free graham crackers, if desired.

Calories per serving: 100 · Fat: 6.5g · Net Carbs: 7.5g · Fiber: 0g · Sugars: 7.5g · Protein: 4.5g

Shortcake Cookie Tarts

Accessory: 7 silicone baking cups · Active Prep Time: 10 mins · Cook Time: 10 mins · Serves: 7

These bite-sized tarts satisfy all the cravings for a strawberry shortcake in a way that is not only portion-controlled but elegant. This gluten-free recipe made from almond flour is a true stunner in its simplicity and makes a big difference in texture and flavor.

INGREDIENTS

Avocado oil spray

1 large egg white

1 $^1/_2$ tablespoons sugar

$^1/_2$ teaspoon vanilla extract

Pinch salt

$^1/_3$ cup almond flour

$^1/_4$ cup almond or coconut whipped cream

$^1/_2$ cup fresh berries

Mona's Tips

Extra-large basket-style or sheet pan air fryers are usually large enough to fit 7 silicone baking cups. Smaller air fryers may require baking these in 2 batches.

DIRECTIONS

1 Lightly spray 7 silicone baking cups with avocado oil spray.

2 In a mixing bowl, whisk together egg white, sugar, vanilla extract, and salt.

3 Fold almond flour into the egg mixture to create a batter.

4 Fill each prepared baking cup evenly with the batter, about 2 rounded teaspoons per cup. Place baking cups in the air fryer basket.

325°F air fry 8–10 mins

5 Shortcakes are finished cooking when they have lightly browned and are puffed up in the center.

6 Remove baking cups from air fryer. Let rest 10 minutes before removing the shortcakes from the baking cups and serving topped with whipped cream and fresh berries.

Calories per serving: 50 · Fat: 3g · Net Carbs: 5g · Fiber: 1g · Sugars: 4g · Protein: 2g

Bananas Brulée with Coconut and Macadamias

Active Prep Time: 10 mins · Cook Time: 8 mins · Serves: 2

The air fryer beautifully caramelizes brown sugar and cinnamon on these halved bananas, which are then topped with coconut flakes, macadamia nuts, and chocolate chips for even more texture and flavor. The best part is that you can air fry the bananas right in the peel for easy cleanup and serving!

INGREDIENTS

1 banana

Avocado oil spray

$1/4$ teaspoon ground cinnamon

1 tablespoon light brown sugar

2 tablespoons unsweetened coconut flakes

2 tablespoons macadamia nuts

1 tablespoon mini dark chocolate chips

Mona's Tips

This recipe can also be used to make cinnamon caramelized bananas, without the chocolate chips, coconut, or macadamias. They can be served on their own or alongside frozen yogurt for around 75 calories per banana half.

DIRECTIONS

1 Leaving the peel on, slice banana lengthwise into halves.

2 Lightly spray each banana half with avocado oil spray and then sprinkle with cinnamon and brown sugar. Transfer to the air fryer basket.

> **400°F   air fry   7–8 mins**

3 Serve each banana half topped with an equal amount of coconut flakes, macadamia nuts, and chocolate chips.

Calories per serving: 195 · Fat: 10.5g · Net Carbs: 23g · Fiber: 3.5g · Sugars: 18g · Protein: 2g

Chocolate Hazelnut Lava Cakes

Accessory: 4 silicone baking cups · Active Prep Time: 15 mins · Cook Time: 8 mins · Serves: 4

The air fryer is the perfect appliance for making a proper "lava cake," as the air flow allows even heat without overcooking the center of the cake. This recipe takes that one step further by stuffing the cakes with chocolate and hazelnut spread to ensure that there will be a lava center, regardless of how long you cook.

INGREDIENTS

Avocado oil spray

$1/2$ tablespoon butter, melted

1 large egg

3 tablespoons light brown sugar

2 tablespoons unsweetened applesauce

$1/4$ teaspoon vanilla extract

$1/4$ teaspoon baking soda

Pinch salt

2 tablespoons unsweetened cocoa powder

2 tablespoons almond flour

4 teaspoons chocolate hazelnut spread

Mona's Tips

For the most "lava" in these cakes, you will want to keep an eye on them and remove them from the air fryer as soon as they start to rise and crack along the top. Start checking on them around 6 minutes into cooking.

DIRECTIONS

1 Lightly spray 4 silicone baking cups with avocado oil spray.

2 In a mixing bowl, whisk together melted butter, egg, brown sugar, applesauce, vanilla extract, baking soda, and salt.

3 Fold cocoa powder and almond flour into the batter until cocoa powder has fully dissolved into the batter. Refrigerate for 5 minutes.

4 Fill each prepared baking cup with around 1 tablespoon of the batter. Place 1 teaspoon of the chocolate hazelnut spread into the center of the batter in each cup before covering with an equal amount of the remaining batter. Place baking cups in the air fryer basket.

350°F   air fry   7–8 mins

5 Lava cakes are done as soon as the tops are set and beginning to crack. Remove from basket to cool on a rack 3 minutes before serving by inverting onto a plate. Garnish with a sprinkle of additional cocoa powder, if desired.

Calories per serving: 135 · Fat: 7g · Net Carbs: 14.5g · Fiber: 1.5g · Sugars: 14g · Protein: 3.5g

Time and Temperature Charts

PROTEIN	TEMP	TIME	RELATED RECIPE
Burgers, 4 ounces each	400°F	8–12 mins	page 105
Burgers, frozen, 4 ounces each	400°F	10–14 mins	page 105
Chicken breast, boneless	375°F	12–15 mins	page 118
Chicken breast, boneless, frozen	350°F	15–18 mins	page 118
Eggs, hard-boiled	275°F	15–16 mins	page 16
Meatballs, fresh	375°F	12–14 mins	page 114
Meatballs, frozen	350°F	14–16 mins	n/a
Pork chops, boneless, 1-inch thick	375°F	10–12 mins	page 121
Pork tenderloin, 1.25 pounds	400°F	18–22 mins	page 77
Salmon, up to 1 pound	400°F	10–12 mins	page 117
Shrimp, fresh	400°F	4–7 mins	page 81
Shrimp, frozen	400°F	5–9 mins	page 98
Steak, 1-inch thick	400°F	9–14 mins	page 110
Tofu, 1-inch cubes	400°F	15–17 mins	page 122
White fish, up to 1 pound	375°F	9–11 mins	page 113
Whole chicken, 3.5 pounds	325°F	60–65 mins	page 126

VEGGIE	TEMP	TIME	RELATED RECIPE
Asparagus	375°F	5–8 mins	page 137
Beets, chopped	400°F	18–20 mins	page 101
Broccoli florets	400°F	10–12 mins	page 90
Brussels sprouts, halved	400°F	15–17 mins	page 136
Butternut squash, chopped	400°F	16–18 mins	page 85
Carrots, baby or sliced thick	400°F	16–18 mins	page 144
Cauliflower florets	400°F	10–12 mins	page 134
Corn on the cob, fresh	375°F	13–15 mins	page 155
Corn on the cob, frozen	400°F	14–16 mins	page 155
Eggplant, chopped	400°F	18–20 mins	page 133
Green beans	400°F	12–14 mins	page 143
Kale, chopped	325°F	5–7 mins	page 28
Potatoes, baby	400°F	22–25 mins	page 149
Potatoes, whole baking	400°F	40–50 mins	pages 146, 147
Radishes, halved	400°F	15–17 mins	page 153
Tomatoes, Roma or Compari, halved	400°F	13–15 mins	page 152
Yellow squash or zucchini, sliced	400°F	8–10 mins	page 81

Recipe Index

Condiments, Dressings, Dips, and Sauces, *continued*

Desserts

Eggs

Mediterranean

Pork

Seafood

Snackertaining

Asian Edamame Snack Mix 60
Avocado Fries with Enchilada Dipping Sauce 67
Buffalo Cauliflower Bites with Blue Cheese Dressing 63
Cinnamon Glazed Nuts 169
Crab Cakes with Remoulade Sauce 68
Crispy Veggie Noodle Nests 140
Everything Bagel Bites 35
Fantastic Falafel with Tahini Sauce 64
Graham Cracker Apple Fries 165
Granola 32
Hard-Boiled Eggs 16
Loaded Sweet Potato Waffle Fries 55
Margherita Pizza Dip 41
Mini Black Bean Tostadas 56
Nashville Hot Chicken Wings 53
Onion Rings with Sweet Chili Sauce 156
Orange Chicken Meatballs 45
Pineapple Ginger Chicken Wings 52
Potato Latkes 59
Roasted Peanuts 49
Savory or Sweet Chickpea Snacks 42
Turkey Bacon–Wrapped Asparagus 46
Zucchini Chips with Lemon and Herb Dip 50

Southwestern

Avocado Baked Eggs 36
Avocado Fries with Enchilada Dipping Sauce 67
Blackened White Fish 113
Fajita Chicken Tacos with Pico de Gallo 94
Mini Black Bean Tostadas 56
Quinoa Stuffed Peppers 86

Spices

Barbecue Spice Blend 11
Blackening Blend 113
Chili Spice Blend 10
Mediterranean Spice Blend 11
Roasting Spice Blend 10

Veggie Meals and Proteins

Air-Roasted Beet and Bean Salad 101
Avocado Baked Eggs 36
Curry Tofu Bowls with Spicy Peanut Sauce 90
Eggplant Parmesan Stackers 97
Fantastic Falafel with Tahini Sauce 64
Italian Shakshuka 15
Meatballs with Marinara Sauce 114
Mini Black Bean Tostadas 56
Quinoa Stuffed Peppers 86
Spinach and Artichoke Frittata 24
The Perfect Burger 105
Tofu Two Ways 122
Very Veggie Quinoa Bowls 78

Veggie Sides

Air-Roasted Asparagus 137
Air-Roasted Beets 101
Air-Roasted Radishes 153
Air-Roasted Tomatoes 152
Avocado Fries with Enchilada Dipping Sauce 67
Baby Potatoes Two Ways 149
Baked Potatoes 146
Baked Sweet Potatoes 147
Balsamic Green Beans 143
Classic French Fries 130
Coleslaw 82
Crispy Brussels Sprouts 136
Crispy Veggie Noodle Nests 140
Curry Cauliflower 134
Golden Corn on the Cob 155
Maple Glazed Carrots 144
Mediterranean Eggplant 133
Onion Rings with Sweet Chili Sauce 156
Potato Latkes 59
Root Veggie Fries with Smoked Ketchup 150
Sweet Potato Fries 131
Veggie Fried Rice 139

About the Author

A graduate of Cornell University in Nutritional Sciences, **Mona Dolgov** is the founder of You Live Right, LLC. As a nutritionist, innovative culinary expert, and publisher, Mona has authored more than 30 cookbooks, developed thousands of recipes for corporate partners, and created patented kitchen appliances. She is also the author of the 5-star rated *The Perfect Portion Cookbook* and the award-winning cookbook *satisfy*. Her scientifically designed recipes provide a balanced and healthier lifestyle without compromise.

Mona also teaches online cooking webinars for medical practices and healthy cooking classes for groups. She is currently a food correspondent for the CBS affialiate WBZ Radio in Boston.

You can find Mona's other cookbooks and join Mona's Kitchen community for even more recipes and interactive classes at:

www.monadolgov.com

@monadolgov on Facebook • **@monadolgov** on Instagram

Mona Dolgov